A BITE OF SOMETHING SWEET

AT CHRISTMAS

BRUCE HENNIGAN

Copyright © 2026 by Bruce Hennigan

All rights reserved.

No part of this book may be reproduced in any form or by any electronic or mechanical means, including information storage and retrieval systems, without written permission from the author, except for the use of brief quotations in a book review.

Cover by ebooklaunch.com

Published by 613media,LLC.

❦ Formatted with Vellum

For Mamaw and Papaw's huge, extended family!

INTRODUCTION

If there was one holiday the Hennigan clan valued above all else it would be Christmas. I have written many blog posts about growing up in the country with my parents and my family at Christmas time. Some of these posts have little to do with the actual day but touch on such things as gifts and snow and cold weather and a loving family. This book is a collection of those blog posts.

At the end of the book there are two very special sections. When my mother, Lena Caskey Hennigan, passed away in 2004, we found a spiral notebook in which she had hand written her life story. I have included the transcript of her story just as she wrote it in this book.

* * *

After my father, Daniel Slayton Hennigan, passed away in 2012 several years passed and Sharon Parker brought me something

INTRODUCTION

one day at church. Her son, Robert, had interviewed my father about his life and had transcribed his story. Daddy recorded his story on a tape. I wish I had that tape! But I do have the transcript and it is included at the end of this book just as he recorded it.

* * *

At this special time of the year, family is so important! My mother and father knew this and they made every effort to bring the family together every Christmas Eve. Now, we try very hard to continue that tradition in their memory.

* * *

So I hope you enjoy the stories in this book. They reflect my mother and father's lives and the ideals they ingrained in our family.

Merry Christmas, 2021
    Updated 2026
    Bruce Hennigan

CHAPTER 1

TRAIN WRECK 1942
Written on December 7, 2011

My father walked through the darkness of the railroad yard. This was not the world he had wanted to live in. But his farm was a bust and my mother had convinced him it was time to leave the country and move to the city of Shreveport and find a job. They had two children to raise; four mouths to feed and the Depression had been devastating on the farm.

When my father and my family came to the city, they moved into a house on Buckner Street along with other relatives. Life was hard but at least working for the railroad, my father had a steady paycheck. The one drawback was the hour. He had the graveyard shift.

Now, he walked through the darkness toward the bus ride back into the city and to home. The railroad yard was filled with hulking, sometimes rusting railroad cars crouched on their tracks. This land was alien to my father, nothing at all like the rolling hills of Saline, Louisiana with its fertile soil and towering pines. His heart raced with anxiety as he stumbled over the tracks and dodged around the railroad cars. And then, the ground opened up beneath him and he was falling through darkness into shadow. He hit the ground and rolled and found himself in one of the maintenance pits over which railroad cars were driven to work on their undersides. He realized if he had hit his head or broken a leg, he might have stayed there until he died. He climbed painfully out of the pit of darkness and despair and resolved to find a better job.

My uncle Marvin was a unique individual. He was tall with a round, cherubic face and a quick wit. When I was a child growing up the 1960's, he would call the house I would say, "Hello?" and he would answer "Is that you?" I was always confused around him. But he worked for the Post Office and the day after my father's fall, he spoke to my father about filling a position at the Post Office. Normal hours. No pits to fall in. Paper cuts galore, but my father could deal with that. He took the job much to my mother's relief. They were NOT going back to the farm!

The holidays arrived and Thanksgiving was a time for true thanks. My father, mother, sister, and brother had a home; food on the table; and my father had a job he could more than tolerate. My father still longed for the farm, but my mother was unrelenting. Once World War II began, their sisters and brothers came through the house on Buckner Street for brief stents as they found jobs in Shreveport. The world was changing. War occupied most of Europe and the country folk were being drawn into the war to end all wars. Fresh faced young men whose life was mostly walking behind a plow and a mule were faced with the prospect of going across the ocean to a world they could not begin to imagine. Shreveport, a growing city in northwestern Louisiana was foreign enough.

The United States was now officially in the war. What would become of our country? What would become of the uncles who were even now being drafted into the armed forces? What would happen to my father? He was twenty-seven when the war broke out. But, because he worked for the federal government at the Post Office, he was not on the first list of draftees. Most men didn't have to be drafted. They volunteered. The attack on the United States was horrific and these men, fresh from the farm, wanted revenge.

In June 1942, shortly after my father turned twenty eight, he was drafted. He was thirty days away from being sent off to Europe. He had thirty days to get his affairs in order; to insure my mother and brother and sister would be okay while he was overseas. At the last minute, with only two days left until he was deployed, the United States government lowered the maximum age of draftees to twenty six. My father didn't have to go and stayed with the Post Office. My uncles were lucky. they survived events like the Battle of the Bulge and came back to the country after the war. But my father tells me the world changed forever on December 7th, 1941. It changed for my family, and it changed for my nation.

In 2005, I immortalized my parents' story in the play, "The Homecoming Tree". It was performed three consecutive nights at Brookwood Baptist Church in November, 2005. It is the story of that house on Buckner Street and the men, women, and children who lived there at the beginning of World War II. It tells the story of a young boy, age 13 and his coming of age when he realizes his father may not come home from Pearl Harbor and he must become "the man of the house". This coming of age is represented by the boy cutting down the family Christmas tree by himself. (I wrote a novel based on the play released in 2016, "The Homecoming Tree".)

In writing, producing, and directing this play, I was able to honor my parents and their extended family and the sacrifice of their incredible generation for our personal freedom. We no longer know what it means to be "the man of the house". Most men today abandon their families to find their personal identity; to discover themselves often in the arms of a younger woman or in the throes of drugs and alcohol. Most families do not resemble the nuclear family of the 1940's. And, it is certain, that most households have no idea of God and country; of self-sacrifice and dying for what you believe in. Truth is, most of us now believe in ourselves and therefore we are dying for ourselves with overindulgence, personal selfishness, lack of manners, rampant consumerism, and would never consider sacrificing our lives for a principle or a value. The exception are those valiant men and women who still understand the necessity of defending the freedom this country still represents, albeit weakly, to a world that no longer regards the United States as a great country.

On this day, the 70th anniversary of the attack on Pearl Harbor, I want to ask everyone to revisit that event; to talk to a veteran; to examine the cost of their ability to sit in front of a computer and have total, unfettered access to a world of information -- true freedom. Freedom is NOT free. It cost thousands their lives on this day seventy years ago. And we must take up the torch of self-sacrifice keep the fire burning if for no other reason than to honor them.

CHAPTER 2

STUFFING? NEVER!
Written for Thanksgiving Day, 2011

Stuffing belongs in cushy chairs, not in turkeys. I grew up eating cornbread dressing and the only thing stuffed in a turkey was those weird turkey parts my mother chopped up and put in her giblet gravy. To this day, I crave cornbread dressing at Thanksgiving. My wife is in the other room right now cooking up her spicy sausage based cornbread dressing and I plan on "stuffing" my face with it Thursday!

My love of cornbread dressing goes way back to my mother's cooking. Each Thanksgiving, my family would travel to central Louisiana to a small town called Saline. There, my grandparents lived in a huge, hulking house that belonged on Universal's backlot tour right beside the house from Psycho. It ached with age; sagging steps; pebbled paint so layered it looked like the gray skin of a huge dragon. The floors were so caked with sand and dirt, you could sweep for days and never get all the grit out of the house.

But no matter how forbidding the house seemed any other day of the year, for Thanksgiving it burst with life and laughter and food. My mother's family was huge, and my mother and her sister had married two brothers, so the Hennigan's and Caskey's celebrated their family reunion together each year. Three tables worth of food would fill the dining room beneath a swaying bare bulb on a long black wire like a vine growing through the far ceiling. And we would gather around my grandparents and pray and thank God for another year and eat all afternoon.

My grandfather had been a deputy sheriff during the Great Depression and had been on the posse that hunted down Bonnie and Clyde. He would tell his stories each year of how each man on the actual posse that shot the criminals ended up dead from alcohol or suicide. Grandmother would sit beside him behind her thick glasses and her easy smile and hair like wild cotton and nod. She was warmth and comfort personified; a short, full woman with a just right hug and a dry kiss.

My grandmother shared one of her memories and when I recall that story, it transcends all the food and the fragrance of yeast rolls and the pebbly taste of cornbread dressing. It never failed, amidst the babble and clanging silverware and laughter, there would be a knock at the back door. My grandmother would painfully rise up from her chair and go out to the screened in back porch. There, she would find a couple of men, maybe an older child wishing her a Happy Thanksgiving. These individuals were well known to the folks of Saline. Today, we would call them homeless. Back then, we called them helpless. And it was the duty of any God fearing Christian to help the helpless.

This was a message I carried away from my grandmother. She passed away when I was thirteen and my memories of her were mostly centered on the kitchen and her biscuits and the great, unwieldy old fashioned washing machine with the hand cranked wringer she used to wash clothes. She was a quiet woman with a deep abiding faith and a slight smile. But, when the helpless would come to the house at Thanksgiving, she did not pity them. She did not send them away empty handed.

During the Great Depression when my grandfather was a deputy sheriff, their family, as destitute as it was, still had much compared to most occupants of the failing farms and drought stricken world around them. My mother would tell me stories of these men, "hobos" and "bums" without work who would pause at my grandmother's back door and ask for a morsel of food. My grandmother would always have something to give these men. Even with eight mouths to feed, she kept something aside. And, when they came by, she would give them food with a glad heart and helping of blessings. Why?

My mother told me many times how my grandmother would looked at her hungry children and explain that these men, these "helpless" in need might be angels in disguise. God might have sent them to test her hospitality; to plumb the depths of her heart to see if she did indeed love the unlovable as Christ had loved us all. My mother, long after Grandmother passed away, would nod and smile and quote this Bible verse:

Be not forgetful to entertain strangers: for thereby some have entertained angels unawares. Hebrews 13:2

My mother has passed on now. My father is 97 and lives in a nursing home where he regularly "ministers" to the residents around him who are in "worse shape" than he by singing old hymns in a loud and sonorous voice. He is entertaining "angels unaware".

I cannot say that I have ever met an angel. At least, not an angel that did not fall from heaven. I have met a demon and I can clearly recall moments in my life when I have been in the presence of great evil. But I have been around many individuals throughout my life who were filled with love and laughter and life. They have encouraged me. They have shared my stories, my pain, and my life.

I often wonder when I meet someone on a trip or on a

foreign soil with whom I seem to have an instant connection if God has sent an "angel unaware" to test me; to plumb the depths of my heart. When I was in medical school a psychiatry professor taught us not to take our frustrations home but to "dump on a stranger" and take out our frustrations on someone we will never meet again. I raised my hand in class that day and told him I could never do that. He wanted to know why and, I am ashamed to admit, I did not tell him.

You see, I can never meet a stranger. I can never meet someone and think poorly of them. For some reason, each person I meet seems to be someone special and unique; a treasure to be discovered; a story to be heard. I owe that to my mother and her mother before her. I am always looking around me for an angelic visit. They taught me well. They taught me the worth of each individual in the eyes of our Creator.

"You may be better off than anyone, but you are no better than anyone."

That is something my mother taught me, and I will go to my grave with it. I will not become cynical. I will not become bitter as I age. I will look at each person fresh and openly knowing that one day, I will entertain an angel unaware. And, for that I am most thankful this Thanksgiving Day.

CHAPTER 3

RECONCILIATION
Written for my Conquering Depression website

My father worked for the post office and Christmas was the worst time for him back in the days before UPS and FEDEX. Every year, he would have to work long, hard hours during the holiday season to make sure all those packages got delivered by Christmas Day.

Our family was strong and close. For us, Christmas Eve became the gathering point each year. My mother and father would welcome my brother and two sisters and their families to our home each Christmas Eve. We would gather and bask in the love we had for each other. My mother was a master of making the most luscious Christmas candy known to man. Our table would be laden with candy, cookies, cake, and dozens of treats. Presents glistened under a real pine tree harvested from our wooded pastures. Often, my siblings would bake chicken and dressing or have sandwiches to accompany the candy. And, always, there was punch!

I look back on those memories with great nostalgia. Now, with my mother, father, and brother gone we still try to gather each year at Christmas and celebrate the love of that Christmas Eve gathering.

But there was one Christmas Eve I wish we could erase from our memory. My father was working late on Christmas Eve, and we could not start our celebrations until he got home around 7 P.M. One of my "in-laws" was hungry on arrival at our house. And, while we were waiting for my father to come home, this person discovered a plate of hot, delicious food placed in the oven to keep warm. They took it out and ate it all!

One of my sisters caught this person in the act and there ensued the cat fight of the ages! The bitterness and anger that filled the air tainted the entire evening. And the hard feelings brought a slight dulling to an otherwise shiny Christmas Eve gathering from then on.

A frequent cause of depression during the holidays comes from these kinds of broken relationships. You know you must see that person at a holiday gathering. Dread fills your heart. Old anger gets stoked in the fires of remembered hurts. Family gatherings can become as welcome as an execution!

How do you handle this? It is time for reconciliation. If you are aware of your depression and you have made a conscious effort to overcome your depression, then guess what? You are a different person! You are a better person than you were last year of the last time you saw that one person you are dreading. Part of what Mark Sutton and I talk about is confronting these kinds of fears and ignoring the old voices of pain from your past. Ask yourself, "What is the lie?"

You see, that person doesn't have to like you. That person doesn't have to change. YOU must change. You must find forgiveness in your heart, or the bitterness and anger will continue to churn up more and more suffocating waves of depression.

Take the high ground. Prepare yourself to greet this person or persons from your past and humbly seek reconciliation. It will not be easy. And you may not be met with kindness. But here is the key. Your CONSCIENCE will be clear. You will find a ton of excess weight lifted from your shoulders.

Tip number one for the holiday is to seek reconciliation. It will be hard. It will be tough. But, if you want to move forward in your battle against depression, you MUST face these ghosts of your past. Not until you've moved past the anger and bitterness can you find HOPE again for the holidays!

CHAPTER 4

*F*UGGITABOUTIT! (2015)

It was a cold Saturday night in Little Italy. This part of New York City was like something out of a 1940's holiday movie. Christmas lights were strung outside each store and restaurant. A glittering lighted star hung across the street at regular intervals. In each storefront window and restaurant window was a Christmas tree; a Santa; a Nativity scene. Each was so genuine, so homemade it made my heart ache with remembrances of Christmas pasts. Dean Martin, Bing Crosby, Rosemary Clooney, and Frank Sinatra singing Christmas songs filled the air. And, to make it all a dream come true, it was snowing!

I sat in Lunella's Italian Restaurant and marveled at the sights and sounds and fragrances around us. Sherry and I had journeyed to New York City for a trip filled with fun and excitement. Sherry and I had never been. But, our friends Magdy and Denise had lived here for years. They had met here and fallen in love here in the Big Apple. They guided us through the streets and filled our minds with wonder and delight.

Nella, the owner of this restaurant, was a tall, willowy

woman somewhere north of seventy with frosted, straight hair and a face filled with smiles. The crowning moment came when she raised her right hand in the air and uttered those famous words, "Forget about it!" when it came time to pay the ticket.

She looked at Magdy who had once worked in her restaurant and said, "I haven't seen you in three years. Can't I give you a Christmas present? So, fuggitaboutit!" It didn't get much better than that!

I discovered some interesting things about New Yorkers. Don't violate their personal space. There are so many people moving down crowded streets shoulder to shoulder I can understand how one woman became very angry that Magdy accidentally brushed her shoulder. She accosted him for not saying he was sorry until she brought the incident to his attention. The argument could have gone on for hours, but I looked her in the face and said, "Hey, lady, get a life. Just forget about it!"

But, once you get past this touchy reaction, they were the nicest, kindest, most accommodating people I have ever met. They put Southern hospitality to shame! Well, all except the driver of the limo from the Addams Family. Denise fell on the subway and cut her knee. It was Saturday night, and we couldn't get a taxi to stop for us. Everyone travels by taxi and considering it was in the twenties and snowing, few people were willing to walk for a long distance. So, Magdy got out into the street and flagged down a limousine. The driver agreed to give us a ride to the hospital. We climbed into an aging, dilapidated limo. Rugs covered the floor and Sherry and I began sinking into the seats. I was afraid the rugs were all that was left of the floor. The interior was dark and there were glasses for having a drink. The problem was they were all cracked and had lipstick and fingerprints all over them. Magdy and Denise got into an argument with the driver over the cost and I just tried to hide in the rugs. Finally, we arrived at the hospital and, I kid you not, the driver got out and he was a twin for Lurch!

But, aside from that the whole trip was delightful. People on the streets actually said, "Merry Christmas" not "Happy Holidays". We had a wonderful horse drawn carriage ride around Central Park. We saw Spamalot on Broadway which was a delight for me, an avid Monty Python fan. Magdy's only comment was, "I don't know what is going on!" which, of course, is the point.

We went to the original Macy's Department Store. The original Bloomingdale's. We saw the new Apple store right across from Central Park. We toured the Empire State Building and saw the Statue of Liberty. We walked around Rockefeller Center and saw the huge Christmas tree and the famous skating rink.

On Tuesday night, we saw the Broadway premier of "White Christmas", and it was incredible! Afterwards, we ate at the famous Sardi's restaurant on Broadway. Magdy knew the maitre d personally. It was astonishing to see over twenty people glare at us as the maitre d hugged Magdy and escorted us past the waiting patrons to our very own personal table! I felt so special. I felt like somebody!

Anyway, the entire trip was surreal and delightful and filled with Christmas images you only see on television or at the movies. But the best was the unending "Merry Christmas" and acknowledgement of the real meaning of this holiday. I guess one of the best moments was sitting in the waiting room of the hospital while Denise was getting her stitches and talking to some native New Yorkers. They were just like me. They were real people with the same kinds of problems that I have. And, they worshipped God and said prayers and looked to a Savior for guidance and forgiveness. They were not some foreign aliens from a strange land.

I will say the strangest moment was when we were selected off the sidewalk to attend the David Letterman show. I have always regarded David Letterman as a strange man with, at times, a very funny show. But, after walking into the historic Ed Sullivan theater the audience was personally greeted by David Letterman. He was real and appreciative of our presence and delightful. He joked with us and thanked us for coming. He said, "We couldn't do this without you. Thank you for being a part of tonight."

An hour later, we were back on the streets of New York City and heading for White Christmas. What a strange world!

So, I hope you have a wonderful, delightful, loving, light filled Christmas. I hope you feel the love of friends and family at this time of the year. I hope that you find the peace, goodwill, and presence of "God with us" that is the central theme of Christmas. I hope you find solace and peace in the presence of the Savior.

And, when troubles come your way, just for this season, say, "Forget about it!"

CHAPTER 5

MY GROWN UP CHRISTMAS LIST (from 2015) One song I always hear this time of year is "My Grown Up Christmas Wish". I decided to make out a "grown up Christmas wish" list.

I wish "they" would let Christmas be about Christmas. It belongs to those who celebrate the Birth of Jesus Christ! That is why it is called CHRISTmas!

I wish marriage was an institution worth fighting for; worth dying for; worth working for again.

I wish we really cared about making the world a better place and not a bitter place.

I wish being in love was less about "me" and more about "you".

I wish we would stop saying "it is what it is". No! It is what we make of it. One person can change the world!

I wish I could still pick up a hitchhiker and not fear for my life.

I wish Superman still stood for "Truth, Justice, and the American Way". Heck, I wish the American "Way" still included Truth and Justice!

I wish there was room in our inns for the baby in a manger.

I wish that what is "true" for me was "true" for everyone as true is true no matter what we think.

I wish young people were encouraged to have ambition and not just pass standardized tests.

I wish Tom Hanks was funny again.

I wish Jimmy Stewart was still alive.

I wish I could climb a tree, not have to save it.

I wish children could still have a childhood.

I wish people would look me in the eye when they talk to me instead of at their phone.

I wish I had a Hobbit hole.

I wish customer service meant serving the needs of the customer.

I wish flying was fun again.

I wish we had a space program.

I wish modern singers stayed on key.

I wish art made sense and didn't involve body fluids.

I wish "tolerant" people were more tolerant of "intolerant" Christians.

I wish Disney still made animated classics instead of buying out all the other companies.

I wish people searching for truth realized He has already been here and can still be found.

I wish the buck at least stopped somewhere.

I wish "smart" phones were only used by "smart" people.

I wish, just once, someone would keep a promise.

I wish movies and books had happy endings. Just a few. Every now and then. Especially when I pay for them.

I wish you a Merry Christmas and a Happy New Year!

CHAPTER 6

"**YOU SAVED MY LIFE**" -- 2018

"You saved my life."

I've heard these words before. Usually, they come from a total stranger through an email or a letter; someone who has picked up "Hope Again" and the LifeFilters and found them an answer to a desperate prayer for help. Let me be honest. I NEVER take such a statement lightly. Every time someone expresses this to me or to Mark Sutton, I am equally shocked and humbled.

This past Sunday, I shared a story with my family at our annual Hennigan Family Christmas Party. I won't detail the story. Just know that the point of that story was to share with my family how a seemingly painful and potentially fatal encounter in my childhood served as the source for something I did later in life that had a profound influence on the lives of others. In this case, four veterans of World War II and an elderly woman who had lived in bitterness for years because of anger over losing her brother in the attack on Pearl Harbor. In both cases, a simple scene in one of my plays echoing that event in my childhood had the unexpected consequence of bringing these people profound peace and reconciliation.

At this time of the year, we reflect on the past. Such reflection can be inspiring, but it can also be painful. Both of our parents are now gone and for Sherry and me, this year is bittersweet. I sifted through old photographs for photos of our parents to place in small picture frames for our Christmas tree. The journey was painful, filled with alternating joyful memories and aching emptiness.

I have to continually remind myself God uses people. True, He uses miracles. But, in the recent centuries, God has used people for His purposes. And most of the time His work takes place through these painful experience in life and through our painful memories. God used my depression to touch people. That is the most humbling thought in the universe. Years of struggling with depression and fear and pain were not in vain. But the key to making those experiences triumphant was giving them over to God for His use. In so doing, I was opening myself up to God using me and my story for His purposes.

This isn't just rambling. That statement I mentioned at the beginning of today's post came from the most unexpected source. I cannot share this person's name. But I will tell you that this person found a package of our LifeFilters left behind by a relative. This person had prayed for God's help with his/her depression and begged for a "miracle". The pack of LifeFilters was left behind "accidentally" at his house by a relative. He/she picked them up and began to use them.

I sat across the table from this person in our church's coffee shop as he shared this with me. It turns out this person had been secretly struggling with the new onset of a type of bipolar disorder. He/she had sought the help of many professionals and was frustrated with his/her response to treatment. He/she looked at me and held the pack of well worn LifeFilters to his/her chest.

"I sleep with them next to my heart every night. They have saved my life." He/she shared how they asked their relative where they had gotten the cards thinking they had to have been written by "some professional from New York" only to discover they had come from his/her good friends Bruce Hennigan and Mark Sutton. I was stunned. I was humbled. This person was an icon to me; a paragon of virtue and Christian values. He/she had taught young students in Sunday School for decades and had changed so many lives for Christ. And here they were thanking ME for "saving my life". Wow! God works in so many mysterious and moving ways!

This Christmas season, we look upon the Nativity scene and most of the world sees it as a great "story". It is recreated in churches and pageants; on Christmas cards and television and in movies. But its more than just a "story". Like every event of our lives, these things really happened and carry with them power and strength for those around us. You see, when God takes our "stories" and uses them for His purposes, they become more than real. They become sacred tools of God's everyday miracles. Like seeing this dear friend of mine clutch a set of LifeFilters to his/her chest like they were a rope thrown to a drowning man.

Many of you are suffering from depression this year. Just know that God is there in every detail and every moment of our lives. Many times, we cannot feel Him; cannot see Him. In our depression and despair, we cry out for a miracle. My prayers for each and every one of you is that God will give you that everyday miracle; that you will find true peace, joy, and hope again in this Christmas season. May God give you peace this Christmas and may you have a wonderful New Year.

CHAPTER 7

S NOWBALL

THERE IS a tense moment in my memory when I was standing on the edge of tall building looking down along the pebbled surface of its wall toward the far distant ground. It is a dizzying and frantic moment for me. I do not like heights. At least not the kind of heights where you can see the building stretching down to the ground. What if out of my entire life I went absolutely insane for ten seconds and it just happened to be the ten seconds I was standing on top of a building and decided I could fly? You understand, don't you?

Anyway, I have no problems with being in a hot air balloon or a ski lift. It must have something to do with the perspective. Or it might be that in a building, there are dozens of people gazing out their windows who would share in your horror as you plummet to your death. It would be repetitive like a scratched record caught on a repeating phrases over and over and over, "Did you see that? Someone just fell off the building?"

I was standing on the roof of the medical school. It was a very dangerous and yet, satisfying place to be. Medical school is so immersive, so consuming, so perverse in its priorities it is a wonder we weren't standing in line to jump. I was fascinated by the fact that security had not locked the door to the roof. Didn't they know what was going through our heads? They saw us drag in every morning tired and dark eyed from studying all night and they smelled us every evening reeking of formaldehyde and death as we stumbled out the door to go home and catch a few moments of uninterrupted sleep. After all, we didn't frolic in every morning with a lilting Irish tune on our lips all bright eyed and bushy tailed!

It had snowed that day. In my neck of the woods, snow was as rare as healthy food at a Baptist dinner on the ground. It had covered the dead brown grass around the medical school with three inches of the white stuff. I went up to the roof of the medical school to see. From the lofty height, I could look out over my city and see it covered with a cold, white blanket of snow. Snow made everything look new and ready for the gift receiver to rip off the paper and find a treasure beneath. It was exciting and calming at the same time.

One of my friends appeared beside me. He was from California where you never saw snow unless it was on a closed movie set. The sky had cleared, and it was the kind of bright blue that hurt my eyes and seemed so impossible it couldn't exist this side of heaven. My friend and I chatted for a while and then he started making a ball with the snow. I had no intention of getting into a snowball fight, but I soon realized he was going to make a huge ball for a snowman. So, I pitched in. There we were reeking of formaldehyde from Ernest, our cadaver, and rolling a snowball across the gravel roof of the medical school. After about five minutes, the ball was over two feet in diameter and pitted with tiny dark rocks from the gravel roof. And that was when my friend got that evil, mischievous look in his eye. It was the same look he had the day he took our cadaver's gender distinguishing parts and placed them on another medical student's female cadaver. This medical student was one of the only two women in our class and she was shocked when she zipped opened her cadaver's bag the next morning. But she never missed a beat and told my friend he had left his privates with his girlfriend.

My friend suggested we take the ball and drop it from the roof and watch it splatter on the ground below. It seemed like a good idea. It is funny how such things always seem like such a good idea at the time. Perhaps it is the adrenaline surging or the presence of peer pressure that makes us utter things like, "Hey, watch this!" We lifted the huge ball of snow and gravel and stumbled over to the wall around the roof and placed it precariously on the edge. We counted down to three and pushed it over.

I will never forget that moment as long as I live. I glanced down and realized we had somehow positioned ourselves directly above the main door to the medical school and just as we pushed the ball over the edge, a person walked out of the door directly beneath the falling snow meteor!

Flash forward two years. I am now a third-year medical student rotating through my clinical wards. I arrived on the obstetric wards with trepidation. I mean, who wouldn't be intimidated about delivering babies? I was immediately placed in charge of a young woman in a coma. Sippy was her name and she lay like Sleeping Beauty on her bed, her arms crossed over her chest above a large abdomen. She was six months pregnant and needed to receive daily intravenous antibiotics for a brain abscess. In order to insure the child growing within her survived, she was admitted to the obstetrics ward. Her mother stayed with her twenty-four hours a day and would only leave on Sunday to go to church. She washed and bathed her daughter and talked to her and read her the Bible and spoke to her unborn child. Soon, everyone on my rotation got to know Sippy's mother and we wished and prayed that Sippy would wake up.

Christmas drew closer and in an uncharacteristic weather event it snowed. I sat in a torn vinyl chair from the 1950's looking out the dingy window in the old section of the hospital at the foot of Sippy's bed. Her mother was reading her the Christmas story from the Bible. I thought I saw movement out the window and I got up and wiped away the grime. It was snowing. The window looked out over the roof of the floor below and already there were two inches of snow. I told Sippy's mother and the residents and interns heard me. Within minutes, they had pried the old window open and climbed out onto the roof. Sippy's mother took my arm and shook her head.

"If my Sippy could just throw a snowball again. What I wouldn't do for that." She said.

I nodded and Sippy's mother suddenly pushed me aside and climbed over the sill out onto the ledge. The interns and residents froze, and I leaned out the window. They looked at Sippy's mother. She bent over and took a huge wad of snow and made it into a ball.

"What you waiting for? It's time to play!" And she turned around and nailed me in the face with the snowball. The snowball fight lasted for almost half an hour, and we were exhausted and happy and Sippy's mother just sat by her daughter's bed, her hair filled with melting snow and with excitement in her voice told Sippy all about the snowball fight.

I WAS on the medical rotation three months later when Sippy delivered a healthy baby girl and Sippy was transferred from the obstetrics ward to the internal medicine ward and back into my care. Her mother stood by Sippy's bed holding the baby and told her daughter goodbye. She had to take care of her granddaughter now. She told Sippy she could go on and be with Jesus. Sippy stopped breathing about an hour later and died.

THE HUGE SNOWBALL was halfway to the ground now and the whole world seemed frozen in time and ice. Like the person below whose life should have been playing out before, I recalled the past.

WHEN MY MEDICAL school classes convened for the first time, we were a shock to the professors. We were the first class in our medical school of over 100 students. All previous classes had been around 33. The new medical school was finished and there was ample room in it for classes of 100. But, as with all good intentions, the plan failed. The new medical school would not be ready until January after our class started in September. And so, 100 students were crammed into a makeshift metal warehouse behind the VA Hospital with our cadavers on vintage Vietnam War gurneys. We named our cadaver Ernest so we would always be working in, wait for it, Dead Earnest.

In these cramped quarters we tried our best to dissect away the dead flesh of our cadavers to learn about the miracles of medical science in the flesh beneath. One day, my friend asked me to walk across the parking lot to the VA Hospital with him. I did and he led me across the foyer and up the elevators to the Intensive Care Unit. In the back corner, we stepped into a room filled with shadows and metal poles and wires all towering over a woman in the fetal position in her bed. Her white hair was as short as mine and her eyes were closed serenely as if in sleep. But her lungs expanded and contracted with rapid vigor. My friend sat by the bed and took the woman's limp hand in his.

"Mother, this is my friend Bruce. We came by to see you." He said. The woman's rapid breathing never changed, and she gave no acknowledgement that she heard her son.

"I didn't know." Was all I could say.

"It's okay." My friend said. "She won't last for long. She wants to be buried behind our church with a full military funeral. She was a nurse in the Vietnam War."

I didn't know what to say and felt like I was intruding on a sacred ritual. My friend looked up at me. "Her family is buried up north. That's where mother should be buried. She said she always wanted to be buried so her grave would be covered by snow on that day. She said it would make the fresh dirt look so much cleaner. But that will never happen in Louisiana."

SEPTEMBER STRETCHED INTO NOVEMBER, and I got the call that my friend's mother had passed away. He would not be in the next day. Her funeral would be at 11 AM. I arrived at the cadaver barn as we called it and started work. After a couple of hours there was a general tumult around me. I looked up from my work and someone had opened the two outer doors allowing us to look out onto the parking lot. I was astounded! I walked down the aisle shuffling past gurneys and medical students bustling about and out into a snowfall. It had just started. A heavy but gentle snow was silently sifting down from a leaden gray sky. I glanced at my watch. It was 11 AM. It snowed for an hour and a half and ended precisely at 1230 PM. I found out later my friend's mother's funeral lasted until 1230 and by the time they had lowered her casket into the ground and covered it, there was enough snow fall left to just barely covered the fresh red earth.

THE SNOWBALL WAS FALLING FASTER NOW and the man below, oblivious to his own imminent death took two steps away from the door and paused. The snowball hit the ground where he had been standing and literally exploded. Snow and gravel splattered for yards around it. I said a silent prayer in thanks that God watched over such fools as myself and my friend and I ran back into the medical school like two kindergartners and back into the arms of dead Earnest.

CHAPTER 8

Rosie: Of Death and Roses

My father was 41 years old on the very day I was born. My two sisters and one brother were almost grown by then and my mother thought she was going through "the change"! Neither of my parents was prepared for the arrival of a new baby so late in their lives. Perhaps my father had forgotten how to play with a child or perhaps he was following in his father's footsteps to be stoic and unemotional around your child. Whatever the reason, my mother's instruction to me each and every day was not to "bother" your father when he "gets home from work." I looked up to the thin, balding man in black rimmed glasses with some trepidation. In fact, there were times I feared him. And so, it was on one particular day at the age of eight I had an odd connection with my father.

. . .

A BITE OF SOMETHING SWEET

WE WERE SPENDING the weekend in the countryside of central Louisiana. There, the rolling hills of red clay were carpeted with towering pine trees and kudzu vines. The journey from Blanchard in the northwestern corner of the state to Saline near the center of the state took two lifetimes it seemed. At age eight, one and half hours easily passed for such an epoch. The winding roads always left me carsick and I had to avoid my cherished M&M's and Pepsi cola until we arrived. But, when we turned right at the stop sign in Lucky just five miles from Saline and I gazed out the rearview window into the distance and saw the towering peak of Mount Driskill, I knew snack time was near.

I OFTEN DAYDREAMED of what lived on Mount Driskill. It was the highest point in the state of Louisiana and the state's only mountain. To my mind, it was Mount Doom with marching hordes of goblins and trolls and the tentacled sea monsters that populated my favorite television show, Voyage to the Bottom of the Sea. I would crane my neck around and rise up on my bare knees in the back seat of our Rambler to watch the mountain disappear in the pine trees behind us. I vowed that one day, I would climb that mountain. One day, I would beat the beasts of hell to the pinnacle and save the world from certain doom! But for now, I had to settle for gingerly turning around in my seat to avoid getting sick and breathing in the fresh air that came in through the open window.

WE OFTEN STAYED with my grandparents in a towering and crumbling ruin of a house filled with darkness and shadows and the smell of ancient sweat. The eaves sagged and sloped down from the huge tin roof. The stairs swayed in the middle as if beaten down by a thousand footsteps. The ceilings inside the house stretched a half a mile into the darkness and one bare bulb hung from this distant roof by a black wire in each room. If you bumped it, the light and stumbling shadows would fill the air with dizzying, swooping stuff of nightmares. I would run out of the room when these creatures descended and hide in my grandfather's outhouse.

TO THIS DAY, I have no idea what possessed my father to ask me to accompany him. He never invited me to go with him anywhere unless it was a family affair. But this Saturday morning was different. I was playing in my grandfather's front yard avoiding the shifting shadow monsters in the house when my daddy came down the stairs and stopped to stare at me. He seldom stared at me. I was only a chance distraction from his piddling and guitar playing and jogging from one end of the house to the other or his jury-rigging of a broken air conditioner or a henhouse wall. Don't get me wrong. I knew my father loved me. He sang to me and laughed at me and always kissed me once in the middle of my forehead every morning before he walked out the door. But, he never really *looked* at me. It was not until I was twenty years old at his brother's funeral that he told me he loved me. But, I knew he loved me as well as I knew the sun would wallow up from its covers each morning and Sootie, my dog, would slobber all over my face when I sat on the back steps and werewolves were real just kept away from our house by my mother's prayers and her bush of switches that could leave red welts on the skin of dinosaurs.

BUT, to *look* at me deep in thought? This was new. I stopped in my tracks and let the three headed monster I was chasing escape somewhere in the distant blurriness of my imagination and stared back. We stood like that in the stillness and the sound of cicadas buzzing and the trees creaking in the wind. A pine cone bounced beside me and I jumped.

"What is it, Daddy?" I whispered.

"Do you remember Mrs. Rosie?" He said.

I blinked. Mrs. Rosie was unforgettable. When we ventured to Saline, my parents always went to church on Sunday. The church was right behind me, across the street from my grandparents' house. It was white washed and made of clapboard with a short steeple and a bell tower. It was not air conditioned and when we went to church, mother always made sure we sat next to a window to catch the breeze. Mrs. Rosie would appear out of nowhere. She was a short, thin woman with wild yellow hair and bright blue eyes. She always wore a purple hat with netting. But, she never pulled down the netting around her face and it flew up over her head like Peter casting his net for the fish Jesus brought to the Sea of Galilee. Mrs. Rosie would hurry over to our pew and descend on me like one of those funny birds that bends at the waist and dips its beak in a glass of water then bobs back up and tilts back and forth. Mrs. Rosie was like that only her nose wasn't covered in felt.

"You are too pretty to be a boy! Isn't he, Lena?" Rosie said to my mother. She would pat me on the head and then reach into her purse. I knew what was coming. It was the only reason I did not hide in my mother's armpit. She pulled out two pieces of Juicy Fruit gum.

"Here you go, young man. You are a miracle from God. Don't you forget it." She would pat me on the head again and then bob up and down and hurry away to her favorite pew.

"Yes, Daddy. I remember Mrs. Rosie. She gives me gum." I said.

My daddy just looked at me some more and nodded. "Well, she has died."

I knew what it meant when something died. I lived on a farm. Animals died all the time. I didn't like it. When my parakeet Cappy died, I cried for two days. When my horned toad died, I didn't know it until it started stinking up the aquarium. When I picked him up he practically crumbled like one of those old mummies. I didn't know what to say to my daddy. It was sad that Mrs. Rosie had died. I would miss the gum. But, she was just one of the many people in my life. Back home, we had 45 cats and 26 dogs and it was sad when one of them died, but there was another one to take its place. Someone else would give me gum.

My daddy looked away then and wiped his face. He seemed to be coming to some kind of decision. He was sweating in the summer heat and beads of water dripped down his bare head into his eyebrows. At home, he would wear a cap with a handkerchief rolled up in the front to catch the sweat. "I've got to go see her family. You should go with me."

I drew in a deep breath. "Go where, daddy?"

"To her house. To console her family." He looked at me. "To tell them how sorry we are Mrs. Rosie has died. It would mean a lot to them if you came. Mrs. Rosie always loved you so much."

"Okay." I said. "I'll go."

Daddy nodded and led the way across the yard to the car. I started to open the back door and he shook his head. "You can sit up front with me."

Sit up front? My face burned with excitement. I never got to sit Up Front. I ran around to the passenger door and hopped up onto the seat. In those days, seat belts were accessories and not required by law. So, I ended up tucking my knees under me with my hands on the dashboard so I could see. It was so different Up Front. As my daddy pulled out of the driveway and into the street, I almost got dizzy! I could see the gray road piling toward us and growing wider as the car ran over it and shoved it behind us. The dashed lines in the center of the road hurtled toward us and each time the car passed over one, I cringed waiting for the crash or the sound of laser fire as if they were energy beams shot at us by aliens.

Daddy was silent as we headed out away from the small town of Saline into the rolling hills covered by the pale green heads of thousands of watermelons. Saline was famous for its watermelons and they were everywhere covering every bare piece of land. They seemed kind of sad to me. It was as if the hills had a million green eyes all gazing to heaven pleading with God to rescue them from the hot, sandy earth; to spare them from being split open with their red meat exposed to the hungry mouths of people.

DADDY PULLED the car off the road and down a dirt driveway to a small, dark gray house. The exterior had never been painted and the wood was gray streaked with green lichen and the dead husks of cicadas. The small front porch was dotted with men and women in their Sunday best. As we climbed out of the car, I began to feel a tremble of fear and anxiety. The people fell silent and their heads turned toward us with terrible swiftness. Some of the women's faces were marred with dark streaks of tears. Some of the men wore frowns and blew smoke into the air. I froze in terror. I didn't know why. These were the same men and women that sat around us in church. But, here on this gray porch in this hot, fetid afternoon they seemed like the very demons of the devil filled with a terrible knowledge, too terrible to share, too terrible to bear.

Then, the moment passed and as one, the people began to move again and speak in hushed whispers and their eyes drew away from me and I was no longer important to them. My daddy spoke to a young woman who glanced at me frequently and nodded as she whispered. Daddy took my hand and led me up the rickety stairs onto the porch. That is the first time I recall my Daddy taking my hand. His hand was dry and rough from working his garden and scaly with dead skin. But, his grip was intense as if he wanted to hold on to me to keep me from being swept away by the people who milled and swayed around us; as if some dark current from some rising river would wash me away.

We stepped into the living room of the small house. The air was thick with the fragrance of roses and six women sat in chairs and on a couch. Their faces glowed with an unearthly sheen. Their eyes bore a deep sorrow and hurt I had only seen in the face of my Sootie the day he climbed up under the house to die. I tried to reach him. But, the timbers that held up the floor of my house were too close to the ground. I could see Sootie's black eyes glittering far in the darkness. He had gone there to die. Alone. Why had he done this? Why would he have to die in the first place? And, why did he have to die away from me? I lay there in the dirt and dust under the house and cried until my sister found me and coaxed back out into the light. Two days later, my Daddy retrieved Sootie's body and we buried him in an old basket out by the pond.

"You must be the little boy Rosie loved so much." One of the women said. It broke the spell of quiet and I swallowed."She gives me Juicy Fruit." I said.

"Do you know why she loved you so?" The lady's eyes glittered with tears.

I shook my head.

"She had a dream that your mother's life was not over and that she would have a child. God told her you would be born. You're a miracle. You were born so late in your parents' lives. She always said you were a gift from God." The woman wiped at her tear streaked face with a lace handkerchief.

Daddy's grip tightened on my hand and I tried to breath. I was a gift from God? Me? This fat little clumsy boy who got sick riding in the back of a car? I looked up at Daddy and tried to loosen his grip. His teeth were gritted so tightly I thought they would shatter. He looked down at me and sighed. His hand relaxed. He squatted down in front of me and studied me from behind his dark rimmed glasses. "I guess I never told you. You are a gift from God, son. Do you want to see Mrs. Rosie?"

I raised an eyebrow in confusion. "You said she was dead."

My daddy nodded. "She is. She's right over there."

I turned and for the first time saw the roses. They were in vases and on stands and on shelves at the other side of the living room around a long, black box sitting on a table. The box was long and shallow and my heart raced. I knew what the black box was. I had seen the same box on television when Dracula had opened the lid to his coffin and climbed out to bring death and destruction to mankind. I took a step back and felt my daddy's hand on my back.

"You don't have to see her, if you don't want to." Daddy said.

I will forever be transfixed in that moment. Eight years old and caught between the world of fantasy and reality, on the cusp of the great opening of my mind to the true world around me, poised on the knife edge of childhood. I could turn and run back out to the car. I could climb back into the back seat and turn my face through the rear window and long to see Mount Driskill. But, a growing sense of inevitability gripped me as if a tight rope was threaded through my navel and slowly, oh so slowly growing taut with anticipation pulling my mind, my soul, my body, my childishness out of the thing it was into the thing it had to become. I took my first step away from childish things, away from the mirror darkly, away from the rain streaked window where Mount Driskill became nothing more than a big hill and the three headed monsters disappeared into simple shadows and the smell of roses became the aroma of death.

I shook my daddy's hand off my back and walked across the

room to the box. I was just tall enough to look over the edge. Rosie was asleep in the dark box. Her hair was perfectly combed beneath the purple hat and the netting. Her lips were red with lipstick and rouge burst forth in crimson from her cheeks and her boney hands were crossed over her stomach. I wanted to feel sad. I wanted to cry like I had when I had seen Sootie. But, instead I was fascinated. So, this is what death looks like? Not some dark phantom of the creaking night with taloned hands and foul breath. It looked like sleep. Like a nap.

I reached out and before anyone could stop me, I touched her hand. These fingers had dug through her purse for the gum. This hand had patted my head. But, the flesh was as cold as an iced watermelon rind. And, I knew there was no life here. Rosie was not here in this room with doting friends and crumbling roses. She was in heaven. She was with God. He would warm her flesh and open her eyes and He would hold her hand as he led her down the streets of gold that we sang about in church.

My daddy took my hand then and pulled me gently away from Rosie. I studied her still features until the edge of the black box eclipsed her from my view and the hot sun greeted my backturned gaze and my father lifted me bodily and put me in the front seat of the car. I do not remember the drive back to the house. I do not remember the road rising up to meet us or the monster emerging from the bushes in the front yard of my granddaddy's house to play with me.

I only remember one thing. The door to my side of the car opened. And, my father reached in with open arms and gathered my stunned body into his grasp and held me close to his warm chest and his beating heart and his firm shoulder as he carried me, crying, up the stairs into the house.

CHAPTER 9

*E*PITAPH
 Written on the 50th anniversary of the Moon landing, 2019

IT'S NOT the Moon landing I remember so much as the time the Apollo 8 astronauts read Genesis 1 while orbiting the moon Christmas 1968. This is a blog post reflecting on the Moon landing and that famous reading of the Bible from the far reaches of space on the day we celebrate God becoming flesh in the Christ child.

On this day in 1969 the newspaper headlines spoke about a massive infantry invasion near Saigon in North Vietnam. 47 enemy combatants were killed with no American casualties. On the same day, the newspaper reported that in the days before Senator Ted Kennedy was pulled from his submerged car and Mary Jo Kopechne, age 29 drowned at Chappaquiddick Island while she was a passenger in a car being driven by the senator. The scandal would haunt him for the rest of his life.

In Bienville Parish, the school board signed off on a desegregation plan for integrating black and white schools. Along the Red River, Shreveport's famous "shantytown" of homeless and indigent occupants was demolished. In other news, plans to implement an anti-ballistic missile treaty with the Soviet Union were stalled in the midst of the height of the cold war. The world was awash with war and possible nuclear annihilation and political scandal and the churning war against the "establishment" by the hew "hippie, free love" movement. America was in turmoil! Soon, oil prices would escalate thanks to the newly formed OPEC and the economy would tank in the aftermath. One of the casualties would be the Apollo space program

But on this day, America had landed a man on the moon. America had succeeded in putting a man on the moon before the end of the decade. We made it by 5 1/2 months!

I was 14 years old and managed to keep my eyes open long enough to watch Neil Armstrong step off the Lunar Excursion Module onto the surface of the moon at around 2 A.M central time. The dark, shadowy image on my television was difficult to discern, but the enormity of that moment was not. I have shared before how my father and I shared a love for the space program. And, the prospect of one day going into space and walking on the moon was always my greatest dream. But here, in a moment of incredible historical significance, all of the bad news of the world around me was vanquished by the deep appreciation of our combined, unified accomplishment as Americans. For a brief moment, millions of Americans put aside their differences and rejoiced in man's ability to reach out for the unknown.

Today, fifty years later, we have not returned to the moon. We have not built the space station seen in 2001: A Space Odyssey. We have not "boldly" gone where no man has gone before. True, we have sent probes and robots to other worlds in our solar system, but we still remain a close, disjointed community of human beings striving to learn how to live together.

. . .

A BITE OF SOMETHING SWEET

TODAY, the strident voices of disharmony and hate are still echoing across our land. The threat of Soviet nuclear annihilation has been replaced by the more sinister cold cyberwar. China no longer threatens us with nuclear weapons but with economic conquest. Our society has not recovered from the postmodern movement of the 1960's and we, as a country, no longer embrace Transcendent Truth but have elevated our individual selves to the seat of godhood.

Shortly after the moon walk, I pondered on the condition of the world I lived in at the time. My view of the future was pessimistic. Little did I know that soon, President Nixon would be embroiled in a controversy that would lead to his resignation. True, the Vietnam War would eventually end but without a victory over the Communist regime we had fought for years. The pain and suffering of our veterans would continue for decades in the aftermath of that war but eventually, they would be exonerated and loved. I have touched the Vietnam War Memorial and nothing so tangible has ever moved me as it has.

I decided to write a poem shortly after the moon walk. Its words were simple but its message clear. In 1972, at the beginning of my senior year, my English teacher encouraged me to submit that poem to a state wide contest. To my utter dismay, I won first place in the state! Somewhere in my closet is a signed copy of a book of poetry by our state poet laureate at the time, whose name has been lost in the dustbin of history. But my English teacher laminated a copy of the poem and the recognition of my award. This was presented to me at my high school graduation and I ran across the framed poem just last week tucked away with a dozen dust bunnies in the back of a closet.

Here is the document in its entirety.

IN THE ANNUAL high school poetry contest, which is statewide, the

BRUCE HENNIGAN

Emma Willson Emery High School Contest, 514 entries were submitted, representing high schools from all over the state.

Northwood is proud to have the first place winner, Bruce Hennigan, an English IV student. We will receive a trophy cup for our school for this honor Bruce earned. His poem is published in the booklet, Louisiana Poets, Volume III, No. 1, March - June, 1973.

EPITAPH

THE TIME-FORGOTTEN *stretches of dust gleam dimly*
　In the intense sunlight.
　Great craterous sores blemish the ashy skin.
　Of the far-reaching desolation and spray
　Reflected light in gushing brightness over the surface.
　Huddled mountains and rocks stand like grinning,
　Laughing gargoyles, a lonely vigil in the silence
　Of vacuous space.
　The pocked, gray surface stares grimly into
　The star-flecked heavens, where in the distance
　A silent green and blue orb, lying upon the
　Black velvet of space like a rich emerald,
　Rises above the pinnacle-jagged horizon
　And peeps sadly at the placid terrain.

IN THE STILLNESS *of many shadows, a lonely*
　Flag stands, its red, white, and blue hues
　Faded across its tattered field.
　Nearby a hulk of corroded machinery
　Crouches on its spidery legs,
　Its many units clogged with dust and
　Faded by the insistent sunlight.

A BITE OF SOMETHING SWEET

On its gray-streaked side a small plaque
Bears these long-forgotten words:
"Here men from the planet Earth first set foot
upon the Moon; July, 1969 A.D.
We came in peace for all mankind."

BATTERED AND ABRADED, *these lone relics of a long,*
  Lost civilization remain, and around about them
  The eternally silent stretches of dust lie
  Quietly like a shroud of death

BRUCE *Hennigan*

MY PESSIMISM at the time stemmed from an America that was changing before my very eyes as it descended into political corruption and postmodernism. My fears were grounded in a world on the brink of nuclear holocaust.

I am not hopeless, however. I am an eternal optimist and my dream was that we, as a people, would overcome these times. The Soviet Union fell. Nixon resigned. The war ended. But as a people we did not cease to change. Many of those changes were good, lasting, long in coming and reflected the true meaning of those words from the Declaration of Independence:

We hold these truths to be self-evident, that all men are created equal, that they are endowed by their Creator with certain unalienable Rights, that among these are Life, Liberty and the pursuit of Happiness.

One of the most powerful statements of basic human rights. Our country was long in waking up to the reality of the foundation it had been built upon. No, WE were long in waking up to the true implications of such a foundation. Even today, we are still foundering when it comes to guaranteeing the basic rights of all human beings.

There is one thing that has always moved me when I recall the space program. During the Apollo 8 mission, the astronauts read from Genesis 1. Buzz Aldrin read from the Bible upon the landing of the LEM on the moon.

I fear that our future is no longer endangered by nuclear annihilation. Rather, our doom is more insidious; subtler and an infiltration our daily thoughts. We have moved into a realm of postmodern relativism and have abandoned any pretense of objective truth or objective morality. We have elevated our individual "selfies" to the level of personal godhood. We no longer look about us at those who are hurting and in need without first thinking of ourselves. Love now equals lust. Sacrifice means putting the smartphone down for a few moments. We have lost the true, grand vision of exploring a universe that teems with evidence for its Creator and in that exploration is mirrored our own desire to know Him.

I fear that this poem may still come true if we do not reverse our moral course and abandon hatred and vile language and narcissistic self-worship.

What will future generations, if humanity survives, think of our space program; of our scientific accomplishments if we abandon basic humaneness? Only time will tell. And, the silent, gathering dust of the moon may be out only epitaph.

CHAPTER 10

DEAD MAN TALKING December 10, 2010

I WENT TO ABILENE, Texas to talk to a man who came back from the dead.

I'll call him Julio. He was a simple man injured severely in a tragic accident that almost cost him his life. I heard the story of the policeman who happened upon the scene of the accident only moments after it took place. They were on a long, dark highway in the middle of flat, empty plains outside of Abilene. They were literally in the middle of nowhere. The officer found Julio lying face down on the side of the road with half of his head caved in and half of his face missing. Julio was not breathing. The officer was convinced he was dead. The man in the other vehicle was unhurt. When the officer went to speak to the other man he noticed someone hunched over Julio.

This new arrival was a man probably in his late twenties in blue jeans and a jacket. The officer ran over to the man.

"Who are you?"

"Just a friend." The man started clearing grass and dirt out of Julio's mouth. Suddenly, Julio gasped for breath and the officer ran back to his car to radio for a helicopter. After the call, he found Julio alone on his back on the side of the road. The "friend" was nowhere in sight. The police officer believes the "friend" was an angel.

I sat across from Julio in a TexMex restaurant just hours after meeting him and hearing his extraordinary story. I had never met this man. He knew nothing about me. I had been asked by my close friend, Mike Licona, to come and interview Julio and evaluate his story and his medical records to see if there was objective proof of his story. Julio had never seen me, never talked to me, and knew nothing about me. Mike had only met him the evening before and during their conversations never mentioned my name or anything about me.

Julio suddenly looked up from his plate and looked over my shoulder as if listening to someone. I turned. There was no one there. He looked back at me.

"What do you have to do with demons?" Julio asked.

I blinked in surprise. "Why do you ask?"

"Dad told me to ask you." He referred to God as Dad. He looked over my shoulder again and then back at me. "And why are you using the number thirteen?"

At this point in my writing career, I was finishing up the final draft of "The 13th Demon: Altar of the Spiral Eye" for Realms. Mike didn't know I was doing this. And, Julio certainly didn't know. I was stunned. "I'm writing a book called 'The 13th Demon' and it is about spiritual warfare."

JULIO JUST SMILED. "Dad said you were doing His work. You need to tell the world all about demons and angels. And, Dad told me to tell you not to worry. You have three guardian angels to protect you."

I got the shivers. I trembled all over and looked over my shoulder. "Where are they?"

"Right behind you. I can see them. You have important work to do and God sent them to watch over you." He went back to his enchilada and acted as if nothing supernatural had happened.

That wasn't the end of Julio's amazing knowledge. But it was both a chilling revelation and also a comfort to know that I had a guardian, no, *three* guardian angels. I have spent a lot of time talking about demons. The word is in the title of my book. But we have to remember that demons are fallen angels. The good guys are still there resisting Satan and his army on our behalf.

Do I believe in guardian angels? You bet I do. In the coming weeks as we prepare for Christmas, remember the first beings to announce the birth of the Savior were angels! Look around you today for the work of God and you just might see an angel or two.

CHAPTER 11

hristmas Trees

MRS. HARTLEY WAS RICH. My Daddy was "leading the singing" at Mildred Crowe Memorial Baptist Church on North Market in the middle of town! Let me explain. We lived in the little town of Blanchard. And somehow my Daddy ended up being the part time choir director of a church almost downtown Shreveport! We were in the Big City! And Mrs. Hartley went to that church.

How do I know she was rich? You should have seen her house. It was spotless. It had furniture I was afraid to sit on! And she had magazines on the coffee table that had pictures of fancy living rooms just like hers!

I was only eleven years old but visiting her house was like going to a queen's palace. One Christmas, Mrs. Hartley invited the choir for a party. My mother made me put on a fancy shirt and wear some dress pants. They made me itch. I'd rather have on my shorts and tee shirts, even in December.

When we go to the house, everyone settled into that fancy

living room. But what caught my attention was this tall, shiny, metal thing sitting in the corner. A light on the floor had this plastic multi-colored disc that slowly spun throwing red, then green, then purple, then blue light across the shiny tree.

I had never seen an artificial tree before. This thing looked like it belonged on "Lost in Space"! I kept expecting Dr. Smith to pop out from behind the tree with a Santa hat on followed closely by the latest monster he had stupidly made mad at him.

Of course, when I begged my mother and daddy to get us one of these trees, they refused. Too expensive! Too shiny! We like REAL Christmas trees. I had to admit it didn't smell like a pine tree or real Christmas tree like the one you could get on the parking lot in front of of the A&P Grocery store.

There is on thing Mrs. Hartley taught me. Just because you're "rich" doesn't mean you're "snooty". She was the kindest and most humble person I had ever known at that point in my life. She always spoke kindly to me and treated my parents as friends.

Maybe one day, when I was living on a space station or flying through outer space, I would have one of those shiny Christmas trees.

HAVING SEEN that shiny Christmas Tree, the following couple of Christmases proved problematic as I wrote in "The Falling Tree". So my mother decided it was time to get an artificial tree. But, it had to look like a real tree.

My mother loved to shop at Atlantic Spartan, the discount chain store where everything was much cheaper than at K-Mart or J.C. Penney. Atlantic Spartan was huge to me. And my favorite section was in the very back — toys! Later, my favorite section was the records and books.

This Christmas, mother and I went to Atlantic Spartan to visit the Christmas Section. It was a delight!

They had about four different types of artificial Christmas trees and one of them looked almost real! But the price! Oh my! I realized that if mother spent that kind of money on this tree, there would be less to spend on presents!

The cheapest tree looked, well, sort of real. The limbs looked like bottle brushes but mother bought it anyway. And there on the shelf by the tree was something else I had never seen. Tiny little Christmas lights. Tiny! The lights we had at home were large bulbs that would heat up over time. Daddy was so paranoid these "hot" bulbs would catch real trees on fire. I tried to imagine what he would think about those large bulbs melting a plastic tree.

But these tiny lights were barely warm! And the colors! Not just red, green, yellow, and blue but maroon and purple and pink. Mother didn't take much to convince her. She bought enough strands to cover the tree.

That Christmas, by the time we covered the tree with these little lights and curtains of shiny icicles, you could hardly tell the tree wasn't real. And, it was straight! It didn't lean to one side. It was not lopsided!

The only problem was it smelled like one of my plastic models! Where was that fresh pine smell? Solution? Mother put a cup of Pine Sol under the tree to make it smell like a pine tree. Didn't really work. But, it did deaden the plastic smell. A little bit.

That got me to thinking. Why not burn some candles in the living room that smelled like a Christmas tree? I consulted with my sister, Sue and soon we were making our own candles! We found kits for making candles with wax and colors to add and fragrances.

One of my favorite photographs from my fourteenth Christmas party shows Sue standing in front of the fireplace leafing through a photo album my mother made for each of us and in the background three candles we had made sitting on the mantle.

Plastic Christmas tree with plastic smell? Solution, make a candle.

* * *

SHERRY and I decided on one of our first Christmases we wanted a real Christmas tree. We went to the nearby tree lot on Youree Drive and picked out a seven foot, perfectly shaped fir tree. We had just moved from our second apartment into our first house. This was before we had children and we happily decorated that tree.

It was around the time of Thanksgiving and we made sure and put the tree in a holder we could add water to. The tree was gorgeous. The tree filled the house with the fragrance of Christmas!

Then about two weeks before Christmas, I walked past the tree and accidentally brushed it. I heard this sudden rush of falling needles. And then it kept on! I stepped back and was shocked to see that an entire section of the tree was devoid of needles. I touched more limbs and more needles showered. We had a huge problem. The tree was beyond dead! It was now a fire hazard!

Sherry and I sat there looking at our dead tree trying to decide what to do. It had to come down. It was not safe. We undecorated the tree amidst showering needles until not only was the tree absent of decorations but also of needles.

What did we do? We bought an artificial tree. But not a bottle brush tree like the one from Atlantic Spartan. No, we bought an expensive tree that looked very real. And for the second time in one Christmas season, decorated the tree!

CHAPTER 12

MYSTERY BOX (2011)

There was the mystery of the man in the rocker. My mother often told the story of how, at the age of 14 (which would be in 1932) she was forbidden by her mother and father to go to a dance party. In the small town of Saline, Louisiana there just wasn't a whole to do for entertainment and my mother really wanted to go to the "Jump Josey" party. So, after she was sent to her room, she slid out the window and ran across the yard in the dark toward the neighbor's house.

She would talk about how much fun she had at the party and suddenly realizing how late it was. So, she ran back to her house. It was now close to midnight and the little hamlet of Saline was quiet and dead as a door knob. She eased up on the front porch with her shoes in her hand and into the house. As soon as she shut the front door behind her, she heard someone rocking in the rocking chair. In the dim interior of the living room only lit by reflected moonlight, she saw someone sitting in the rocker. Her heart was beating and she was so afraid it was her mother and father. She quietly slipped by the chair but when she passed her parents' bedrooms, they were both in the bed fast asleep. All of her sisters and her brother were in their beds. Then, who was in the rocker?

This was the great mystery. I remember sitting on the edge of my seat as my mother told this story. She told it over and over throughout my childhood. And, I jumped every time the big Reveal was, well, revealed. In fact, my mother and father were incredible story tellers. It seemed as if their entire lives were one unending story after another. I grew up believing in fairy tales and ghost stories and that good would always triumph over evil. I grew up believing that life, like stories, has a beginning, a middle, and an end and the best stories always have the strongest endings! I grew up believing that everything in life was a story; coherent; understandable; forward moving toward a satisfying end.

In our postmodern culture where relativism rules supreme, it is difficult to see where life in the 21st century matches the classic story. I guess that is why I absolutely LOVE anything written, directed, or produced by J. J. Abrams. Yes, I watched every episode of LOST with breathless anticipation. And, yes, I loved the finale. It fit. It was inevitable. It was a strong ending. I watched every episode of Alias. I went back and watched Mission Impossible III again and loved it. And, Fringe is one of my favorite shows right now. And, as a life long Trekker, I was shocked and stunned by the brilliance of his reboot of Star Trek. J. J. talks about how in each story, there is a Mystery Box. He has a box given to him by his grandfather he has never opened. What is in the box? It's a mystery and the story is all about discovering the mystery in the box.

My mother gave me a "mystery box" each and every time she told me that story. It set the stage for my entire life. It has made me an investigator of all around me: people, places, things, situations, life in general. For in every one of us, in every situation there is a mystery to be solved. And, it is in the journey to discovery that life finds its most satisfaction for me. In fact, the greatest discovery of my life was in finding a relationship with Jesus Christ. Opening that "mystery box" was the most profound experience of all.

Oh, yeah. The rocker.

My mother slowly crept back into the living room, still carrying her shoes. The rocker was still but as she got closer, it began to rock again and she could now hear a deep, throaty breathing from the person in the chair. Who was it? Had someone come into the house to rob them? She should have run back to her parents' bedroom and cried for help, but if she did, she would be in big trouble over the dance. So, she drew nearer to the chair and asked, "Who's there?"

More deep breath and now, a thumping sound like a heart beating hard and slow. She reached out in the darkness and felt hard, scratchy whiskers and she screamed, throwing her shoes up in the air. The man in the chair bolted up and landed right on top of her as they toppled to the floor. The man's face grew close to hers and he licked her. He licked her? The lights came on as the family tumbled into the living room and there perched on top of my mother was the family hound. You can figure out the rest!

CHAPTER 13

WHAT EVER HAPPENED TO MR. POTTER?
A short story about the fate of Mr. Potter after the events in "It's a Wonderful Life"

The jail cell was cold and dank. Someone had forgotten to replace the light bulb and only a few strand rays of limpid light fell through the barred window. Even through the thick, ice-covered glass of the window, the man sitting in his wheelchair could hear the revelers outside. He snorted and sniffed in anger as he tried to ignore the voices raised in song and celebration.

He rubbed an arthritic hand over his pale face, massaging his downturned mouth. He blinked his heavy eyelids and peered into the dark shadows of his cell for any sign of relief.

"I want to speak to my assistant, do you hear?" He bellowed, not for the first time. His words fell on deaf ears, swallowed up by the cold indifference to his very existence. "Do you know who I am? I'll have the sheriff throw every one of you in jail!" He grabbed the wheels of his chair and tried to push himself toward the door to his cell. It was a dark, rust stained metal door with a barred window too far above his head to do him any good. He gasped for breath as he tried to push his chair closer. He was not used to moving his own chair. His assistant pushed him everywhere. He realized this was a sign of weakness. He should never have become dependent on another human being!

He came within an arm's reach of the cell door and banged his fist against the metal. It was cold and rough with bits of rust. "Let me out of here, I tell you! I own this town! I own the sheriff! I'll foreclose on every one of your houses, you vermin!"

A shadow eclipsed the wan light coming from the hallway and a face appeared in the window. "Sir, you need to be quiet or we will have you physically restrained."

The old man squinted toward the window. "This is outrageous! Let me out of here!"

"I'm sorry, but you have been arrested for theft."

"I want my lawyer." The old man wheezed and began to cough.

"It's Christmas day. We can't find your lawyer." The man in the window said. "Can't tell you how good it makes me feel to see you in this jail cell. I was telling my friend, Ernie, how wonderful it was to actually arrest you and throw you in this cell! Let me ask you something. You own the bank. You own every business in town, but one. Why would you throw all that away by stealing $8000 from one of your own bank customers!"

"It was a mistake, I tell you." The old man wiped tears from his cheek as his coughing session finally ended. "I found that money in my newspaper."

"Found $8000 just lying around tucked inside your newspaper? Who in their right mind would let something like that happen?" The man in the windows asked.

"That crazy old accountant, that's who. He's lost most of his mind. He's daffy!" The old man pointed a gnarled finger at the window.

"Oh, so you saw the accountant put the money in your newspaper? If you didn't want to steal it, why didn't you tell the accountant he had misplaced his money? Seems to me, you saw a chance to steal something you could never get your hands on, and you took it. And, I'm not talking about the money. I'm talking about the business."

"I know what you're talking about! I swore out an arrest for the real thief and he should be in here instead of me. Now, go do you job and arrest him and let me go."

The man in the window pulled away and the old man heard another voice in the hallway.

"Bert, I want to talk to him." The old man recognized the voice immediately and his face grew hot with anger.

"George, you should go home and be with your family." Bert said.

"I need to talk to him, Bert. Just a few minutes."

The old man wheeled himself painfully away from the door and grit his teeth. How should he handle this? He could still get the upper hand. If he planned this carefully! The door grated and opened. A tall man stood silhouetted against the light in the hallway and his shadow stretched across the jail cell and covered the old man in darkness.

"I suppose you've come here to gloat?" The old man said. "Well, you can just turn around and go back to your scruffy little family. I'll be out of here in no time and I plan on launching a law suit against you and your firm that will finally crush your building and loan business."

George stepped into the room and moved to the side to sit on the room's only piece of furniture, an old Army cot. He held a fedora in his hands and he placed it on his knee. He wore a nice suit with some fraying of the threads along the lapels and a jaunty tie with red and green bows on it. He wiped at his long face and blinked.

"I know that I should just sit here and soak all of this in. Imagine. The great Mr. Potter sitting in a jail cell. Who would have thought such a thing was possible?"

Before Potter could open his mouth, something exploded against the outside window. Potter jerked and George glanced over his shoulder. Red pulpy flesh dripped down the outside of the window.

"Waste of a good tomato." George said.

A voice echoed from outside the window. "I hope you rot in that cell, Potter!" Other voices joined in, rising in volume, blending into a cacophony of cursing and threats. A whistle interrupted the voices and Bert's voice was heard ushering the mob away.

"I suppose you put that unruly mob up to this, George. I'll add that to the law suit." Potter growled.

George sighed. "Mr. Potter, I don't have to say a word for the people of this town to rise up against you. You've held so many things over their heads for so long that now you're locked up, they realize you can't hurt them anymore. No, I don't have to speak a word. You are your own worst enemy."

Potter rubbed his hands together. "Well, I guess you've finally won, George. So, I'll tell you what I'm going to do. I'll speak to the bank board and the city attorney about this mix-up in the money and have them drop all the charges. I'll even forget the law suit. You can go on taking care of your unruly mob of friends and I'll get back to the real business of running this town."

"And, the $8000?"

"You realize it was your own dim-witted uncle that lost that money?"

"And, it didn't take you long to find it, right?" George said. "Mr. Potter why didn't you just call up my office and tell me what happened? We could have avoided all of this."

"George, your building and loan has been a pain in my backside for years. And, suddenly, I was handed the very tool I needed to bury you." Potter smiled. "I did nothing wrong, George. It was all the doings of one of your employees. He lost the money and your business should have gone under. I refuse to back down from that. But now that you have beaten me, George, I'll give in. I'll put you on the board of directors of the bank and award you a sizable portion of the stock and bond options. You can finally have enough money to get everything you want. What do you say?"

George smiled. "Mr. Potter, last night I almost threw away God's greatest gift to me, my own life. He showed me that the most important thing in this world is not money or stocks or bonds or positions of power. It's people, Mr. Potter. Friends and family whose lives have intersected with mine. God has used this measly little old building and loan clerk to change the world, Mr. Potter. And, you want to hear something amazing?"

Potter raised an eyebrow. "Do I have a choice? Go on with your sentimental hogwash."

"He used *you*, Mr. Potter. You were part of this grand plan of His, too. Now, when Bert handed me this bunch of papers a while ago," George pulled out a folded bunch of documents from his inner coat pocket and tapped them against his leg. "I was understandable elated. You see, Mr. Potter, the board of directors of the bank met this morning and stripped you of everything. Yep, met on Christmas morning, that's how elated they were to be rid of you. You are no longer the president and owner. They seized your stock and bond options. Then, the bank turned over all mortgages and loans to me. Imagine that, Mr. Potter. The world has turned upside down. I'm in charge of this town now. Not you."

Potter gasped and his face grew pale. "I don't believe a word you're saying."

George stood up and placed the papers in Potter's lap. "See for yourself, Mr. Potter. You're finished, kaput, gone with the wind. You'll spend the rest of your life right here in this cold, dank jail cell. Even your own assistant turned against you and right now, the sheriff is searching your home for more hidden skeletons in the closets."

Potter grabbed the papers and squeezed them tightly as veins stood out on his forehead. He hurled them aside and they separated in the air, raining down on the floor in a gentle susurration. "You scurvy little rat! This is far from over, Bailey."

"I'm afraid it is, Mr. Potter. I'm afraid it is. Now, if you are interested in turning your life around, all you have to do is say a little prayer for help and my friend, Clarence will help you gain a new perspective on your life." George walked toward the door.

"Who's this Clarence?"

"An angel, Mr. Potter." George paused and looked around the cell. "There is one thing you were right about. I came here to gloat. But I realize I've been given a second chance at life so I can't hold anger and bitterness against you anymore. Mr. Potter, I forgive you."

"Forgive me? How dare you!" Potter sputtered.

"You might want to consider asking for forgiveness for yourself. Because, when I close this door, either you'll spend the rest of your days with an angel. Or," George slowly closed the door until only his face could be seen through the tiny door's windows. "you'll spend it with your own private demons. Merry Christmas, Mr. Potter."

Potter opened his mouth to respond as George disappeared. He glanced around at the dark shadows of his chamber. "Me, ask for forgiveness. Never!" He screamed. "Do you hear me, never!" His voiced echoed into silence and through the window he heard the voices of people singing Christmas carols. "Never!" He whispered.

The papers stirred around his feet and something moved in the blackest corner of his cell. He peered into the shadows and two tiny red eyes blinked.

"Seasons Greetings, Mr. Potter!" a raspy voice echoed

through the chamber filling Mr. Potter's heart with an unfamiliar sensation, dread.

CHAPTER 14

SEANISMS

9/17/1987

Yesterday at the supper table, Sean (out of the blue, of course) stated, "Dad, I want some of those shoes for Christmas."

"What shoes?" I asked.

"You know, those shoes for you to walk on the wall with."

I looked at my son strangely. "And, where do I go to find these shoes? Who showed them to you?"

"Well, Pee Wee Herman had them on his feet."

I love my son so much! I see him when he looks off into space and I knew he's just thinking! He is so sensitive to everything that is said around him and he worries. I want him so much to know I love him and that he is very special and, most of all, God will take care of him as well as our whole family. Even if he never walks on the wall!

9/19/1987

From the bath tub, Sean said. "Before I go to bed, Dad, I want to count the stars."

"Count the stars?" I asked.

"Yes, like Goose did in Rest, Rabbit, Rest. After I take my bath, I want to count the stars."

What a testimony to the power of God to look up at that vast sea of stars that demonstrates His goodness. Sean assured me that each one was made of "hot and shining gases."

Oh, yes, scientist will have to rewrite their textbooks. Sean counted 20 stars!

9/26/1987

Last night, all of us were in the playroom. Casey is just beginning to crawl, a thing Sean never did. In many ways, she has more mobility at this early age than Sean did.

In a flash of silliness, I put Sean's yellow helmet on Casey and he responded, "Look, Mom. Casey is a flying squirrel." He was referring to my tee shirt that had Bulwinkle and Rocky, the flying squirrel on it.

10/31/1987

Sean, last night at Italian Gardens, told me he was "full right up to the top of my head. See, that's why my head is so hard because it is full."

11/4/1987

Sherry had strep throat and I went to the hospital and got her a shot of penicillin. This is what Sean said, "Daddy, I need my doctor kit to go with you to the hospital and then I will check Mommy's ears and feel her tummy."

At the hospital, he repeated all of this to the ER ward clerk and told her when he grows up, "I want to be a doctor like Daddy." I never prompted this attitude in him. He arrived at this desire unsolicited. And, frankly, I want Sean to be the person God intends him to be, doctor or not.

Late 1987

Sean stayed with my sister, Sue, while Sherry and I went on a couples' retreat. He was crying when we got home. "I need more hair!" because Sue told him to stop playing with his hair or he would pull it all out. He has stopped playing with his hair.

Last night, Sean asked me why I was growing a beard and then answered his own question. "Sometimes a daddy has to grow his whiskers real long."

Sean said, "When I grow up and get big, I can sleep in the bed with you and Mom. And, then when I get married my wife can sleep with us, too."

5/27/1988

In the back yard, Sean found earthworms crawling out of the ground. He picked them up and kissed them. Appalled, I accosted him about his actions. His reply, "Because they are my friends who keep the grass growing."

I was very upset about something and Sean said, "Just calm down, Daddy, and you can help me color."

CHAPTER 15

A MOMENT WITH MARY (2016)
I was asked to write a monologue from Mary's memories for Brookwood Baptist Church's event, "Joy". Now that it has been performed, I want to share it with you on this first day of December as we count down the days until we celebrate the birth of our Savior.

A Visit With Mary

Mary is sitting on a stool that looks hand made. She is sitting beside a table and picks up a hand carved animal and seems to study it.

No parent should ever have to bury their child. Ever. When you hold your newborn baby, you never imagine the end. You only think of the beginning. All is fresh and new and tomorrow is forever.

She puts the animal back on the table.

I heard about my new baby from an angel. Really! You don't believe me, but that is just fine. An angel told me I was going to have a baby boy and even told me what to name him. I couldn't tell just anybody. They would think I was crazy. After all, I was so young, so innocent and already engaged to be married. Yeah, engaged.

My husband was a good man. Hard working. Dedicated. Loved the Lord. He didn't tell me about his angel until he was dying. Told me an angel visited him and told him to marry me no matter what. He listened to the angel and he listened to his heart. He loved me. And, I loved him. He was such a good father.

She picks up the animal again and paces as she talks.

There was that time we lost my son. We were traveling and you know how you always have this fear that your child will wander away and get lost. I mean he was 12! And granted a 12-year-old should be responsible. But for days we thought he was playing with the other boys only to discover we had left him behind in the city! I should have known he would be different. What kind of child comes with the birth announcement of an angel? He wasn't hanging out with the other boys. He was in the church talking to the heavy thinkers; you know, the philosophers, the historians, the theologians. And here I'm going to have to be a little proud and not so angry when I tell you that he was more than carrying his own weight. Some of these very intelligent men were astonished at what my son knew.

Mary goes back to the stool and sits down. She places the animal on the table and becomes very thoughtful.

Of course, his brothers and sisters never really liked him that well. They all knew he was different. That's why that time at the feast I tried to stop them. They thought he was crazy. I tried to explain that their brother was not crazy; he was not delusional; he was special. God had His hand on my son but they insisted on confronting him and the words they spoke about their brother! I can't tell you how many times since then they wished they could take those words back. When you've said something so hurtful to someone you love and then they die, well, you can never find peace again.

Mary suddenly grows very proud of her son and motions to the table.

I have this table, right here, see? It is small and not exactly perfect but my son built this for me right after he turned thirteen. And, this stool I'm sitting on he made when he turned twenty. But, all of his glorious skill with working with wood ended when he turned thirty. He stopped shaping the hearts of trees and began to shape the hearts of men.

My husband once told me that a man should be happy if he has raised someone smarter than himself or more successful than himself. He never had the opportunity to hear our son speak. Such words! I once watched him carving a limb -- an old, gnarled piece of driftwood from the sea of Galilee.

He started out just looking at it and studying it. And then, he began to cut away the dead twigs and strip away the rotten flesh. And, then he exposed the beautiful swirling pattern of the heart of the wood. He polished it and sanded it and coated it with oil and wax until the limb became a beautiful walking stick for my father. How did he see what was inside that broken, gnarled and discarded piece of wood? Only the Lord could show him the potential of what lay inside. He is that way with words. He sees into the hearts and minds of men and women and the words that cut to the quick; that expose the hurt; that sooth the pain; that heal the wound; or they prick the recalcitrant heart and those words are sharper than a two edged sword. He is the word. Yes, the very word of God.

And, yes, it would be His words that brought about his downfall. The wrong words were spoken by his brothers and they hurt him. But the right words were spoken by my son and they killed him.

Mary looks up as if looking at Christ on the cross and hugs herself in pain.

I was there when he hung on the tree, irony of ironies he should die on the very wood he spent his life shaping. My heart was broken and I remembered the first night I held him; cold, wet; crying and hungry as angels filled the night and shepherds bowed at our feet and the skies sang with a thousand hosannas.

She unfolds her arms and gestures to the "cross".

But where were they now? Where were the angels as he bled on the cross? Where were the lowly shepherds who fell at his feet? Where were the songs of praise and triumph?

They were gone. The angels, like his heavenly Father, turned their backs on him in his hour of greatest need. The shepherds did not bow at his feet but hurled insults and bitter hatred and cried "Crucify Him." And the songs of praise were replaced with a silence so profound, so deep it covered the earth with its sorrow.

Mary stumbles back in pain and sorrow and sits roughly on the stool. She mimes the action of them placing Chris in her lap. As she talks, she touches the wounds on his head, touches the wound in his side, touches the wounds on his hands.

I held him in my lap just as I had as a baby. He was cold; wet; but he no longer cried and he no longer hungered. His lifeless body sucked the very life out of the universe; the creator born of my womb; drinking from my body, now limp and helpless in my arms. God had been born. God had died. And, I had been the bookends of His life.

Mary relaxes and turns back to the table. She picks up the carved animal again.

I am waiting now. Waiting for a great and glorious reunion. I was at the empty tomb! I saw my Son reborn; in new flesh still marred with the scars of his atonement. He walked among us for days and then bid us goodbye to become one with his Father. I miss him greatly whenever I touch this table or hear this stool scrape across the stones.

She closes her eyes, holds the toy animal to her face and inhales as if remembering. She opens her eyes and begins to talk.

Every now and then, I catch a glimpse of Him out of the

corner of my eye or smell his fragrance on a chance breeze for His is the breath of life; His is the everlasting water; His is the Life eternal to give to us all. I have had a good life. I have had a life no mother could ever have imagined. It all started with an angel visit and it will end with my Son coming for me. He will welcome me into His arms only I will not embrace Him.

Mary falls to her knees and kneels as if at the feet of Christ, looking up in wonder.

No, I will fall at His feet in worship and praise for my son who was born to die, died so that we might live forever!

CHAPTER 16

*T*HE NIGHT I KILLED SANTA
They found him in an abandoned warehouse just two weeks before Christmas. He was alone, dressed in a Santa costume. (Of course, this man wasn't REALLY Santa!) He was in a coma. He had no identification on him. I first saw "Santa" in the emergency room shortly after he had been admitted to my internal medicine team. His blood glucose was 32. Normal is anything above 90 and less than 120. When you get below 50, you're approaching a comatose state. We had no idea how long he had been like this. I chose to admit him to the intensive care unit until we could get him stabilized. Shortly after bringing him to the ICU from the ER, he coded -- medical jargon for cardiorespiratory arrest. In other words, his heart stopped and he died. We worked on him for a good hour and managed to get his heart beating again but he had trouble keeping his blood oxygen level up so I decided to put him on a ventilator. It was the last free ventilator in the hospital.

That was when the fun began. Let me elaborate.

Bed 1 contained a man weighing 780 pounds. We tied two hospital beds together to hold him. He had been admitted to surgery for removal of a hernia so large, he had carried it in a wheelbarrow. But the surgeons had no idea how to maintain the fluid balance of a 780 pound man so he developed fluid on his lungs. He coded at this moment and my team of medical students and the other intern starting working on him. I remember one of the medical students literally perched on the huge man's chest pumping on his heart with her knees!

Bed 2 contained a man with delirium tremens. As soon as Bed 1 turned south, the man decided to pull out his Foley catheter without deflating the balloon. He was whirling the catheter with its balloon the size of a grapefruit around his head like a lasso while chasing one of the nurses. He was spewing bright red blood from his, uh, privates all over the floor.

Bed 3 contained a prisoner from the local jail. He had "overdosed" and was now in a "coma". He had been in a "coma" most of the day although we suspected he was faking it just to stay out of jail. He had overheard me talking to the psychiatrist earlier saying as soon as he woke up, instead of admitting him to the psychiatric ward for treatment of his "depression", we would send him immediately back to jail. In the developing chaos, he woke up, opened the window and climbed out on the seventh-floor ledge to "kill himself". He was going to prove he was suicidal so we would have to send him to the psychiatric unit and not back to the jail.

Bed 4 contained a medical student in her mid-twenties. She had "converted" her PPD, meaning that sometime since starting medical school she had been exposed to tuberculosis and her skin test proved it. She had been placed on prophylactic medication which had proceeded to destroy her liver. She was currently experiencing "hepatic encephalopathy" meaning she was delirious from all the ammonia building up in her bloodstream from her failing liver. She started screaming at the top of her lungs and trying to tear out of her restraints.

Bed 5 contained an elderly woman dying from ovarian

cancer with fluid buildup in her lungs and her abdomen. Her protein was so low in her blood, we had to keep her in ICU to build her protein back up. She was on a ventilator.

Bed 6 contained a man recovering from a massive heart attack. As our CCU, or cardiac care unit, was full, he had been moved to the ICU and was also on a ventilator. He was only 38 and currently sedated so he wouldn't fight the breathing mechanism of the ventilator.

Bed 7 was currently empty.

Bed 8 contained Santa.

The next two hours were the most chaotic I have ever experienced in my many years of medicine. The 780 pound man died. The fellow in DT's slipped on his own blood, fell and was taken to surgery for a subdural hematoma, a blood clot on the brain. The medical student began vomiting blood and we had to call in the gastroenterologist to try and "scope" her and find the source of bleeding. The psychiatry resident closed the window on the prisoner after telling him if he was still on the ledge in the morning, we would send him back to prison assuming he didn't freeze to death. Otherwise, he could climb back inside and get sent back to prison without frostbite.

It was now 3 in the morning and I went to check on Santa. His status had not changed. He had not awakened. We still had no idea as to his identity. It was then the next admit rolled into ICU, a young woman in diabetic ketoacidosis. This is a state where the blood sugar is so high the patient becomes delirious and is in serious danger of dying. To top it off, the young woman had developed a rare complication, ARDS. This affected her lungs which were filling up with a proteinaceous material. If we didn't get her on a ventilator soon, she would die.

But there were no ventilators left in the hospital! That meant I had to make a decision.

In that day's medical environment, most people don't realize the loneliness of being the doctor on the spot. We are trained to make these kinds of decisions; to weigh life and death scenarios in a split second. Our current medical environment has taken that choice away from doctors and placed it in the hands of administrative individuals whether in the government or with an insurance company. These faceless, sterile, uncaring individuals sit behind a computer screen scrolling through a "cookbook" of these scenarios and deciding whether or not the doctor can make the appropriate decision only the doctor is trained to make. But, back then, the doctor was the final decision maker. The doctor, whether he liked it or not, was God.

I stood there faced with the inevitable prospects of taking a ventilator away from one of my patients. Who would it be? And, I had to make the decision quickly. For the young woman to survive, someone would have to die. Who then?

I stepped into Santa's cubicle. He was still wearing the red pants and his long white beard covered his bare chest as it rose and fell with the ventilator. I shooed the nurses and medical students out of the room. This would be my decision and mine alone.

"Sir," I said. "I do not know your name. I know nothing about your past. I have no idea why you were in that empty building dressed as Santa. The only thing I know is that I have to make a decision and, I'm sorry, but it is time for you to die. I know that God knows your mind and your heart and I only hope He ushers you into heaven with open arms. The only thing I can offer to you is that although you may have spent your last waking moments totally alone, you will not die alone. I will be here with you."

I turned off the heart monitor and slowly removed all the wires and EKG patches. I pulled his red Santa coat up and buttoned it over his chest. I removed the IV lines from his arms and straightened his long, white beard down over his chest. He had been wearing a tiny set of reading glasses in the warehouse, and I put those gold hued glassed back on his nose. For all the world, he looked like a sleeping Santa Claus save for the tube coming out of his mouth. I reached over and turned off the ventilator and slid the tube out of his throat. The respiratory technologist whisked the ventilator away and I reached down and took the man's hand in mine. I felt for his steady pulse and waited as it slowed until it vanished.

I will never know who this man was this side of heaven. I will never forget the pain of making that decision even now 42 years later. I would never forsake another human being in the moment of death. We come into this world alone and are instantly embraced by family. But death is a lonely experience. Even surrounded by loved ones, only we can experience the ultimate journey. But we are not alone. God sends his angels to usher us into heaven. I have heard so many stories of men and women seeing the divine at the moment of death. There is that comfort.

The night I allowed "Santa" to die so that a young woman could live, I learned the most powerful lesson in the world. It is the lesson of Christmas. It is the heart of the Nativity story. It is the fulfillment of man's journey through darkness and evil. It is this. Someone had to die so that we could live. Jesus was born to die. The babe in the manger was overshadowed by the cross from the moment he drew his first breath.

This Christmas season, pause and look around you. Notice the unnoticed. Feed the unfed. Bless the unblessed. Love the unloved. Find the babe in a manger that cries in hunger. And, ultimately, share a love that is so profound, so deep, so unfathomable that because of that love He drew a cold breath in a manger only to breath His last breath on a cross for all of us.

CHAPTER 17

*H*OW I BECAME CAPTAIN AMERICA (2012)
This is how I became Captain America.

It was late on a Tuesday and I was slaving over the Christmas gift for my mother. It was the most difficult handmade gift I had produced in my long life of eleven years. At our Cub Scout meeting, we were making trays for our dear mothers to serve us food and drinks on. Mr. Talbert had cut out round wooden slabs with white Formica on them and our job was to staple rope around the edge and make two rope handles at opposite sides.

Although I did know it at the time, after my mother received the gift, she discovered the handles were slightly off center and every time she would load up the tray and pick it up, one side would tip downward and glasses of lemonade would fall to the floor. Jelly glasses of lemonade. We drank out of glasses from jelly jars.

My mother was the original master of recycling. She would take everyone's drink left at the end of a meal and pour ice and all into a large glass and then DRINK it!!!! The original Suicide drink!

Back to the tray. I was upset. I was chagrined. I was ashamed. My mother's gift was useless. In a temper tantrum I jerked all the rope off around the edge and jerked off the handles and then threw the thing across the front yard. Amazingly, it sailed through the air like a giant, fat Frisbee, bounced off of a tree and imbedded itself edge down into the dirt.

I gasped. I raised an eyebrow. I chuckled. I had a shield! Just like my hero, Captain America. I ran into the house and dug through a drawer until I found the black, red, and blue Magic Markers. I was a student of math so I wanted my concentric circles to be perfect and my star to be just right. So, I took out my compass and some string and a ruler and I marked off the rings and drew the star on the slick white surface of the shield. Then, I colored in the red rings and the blue background for the white star. I cut some leather straps from an old belt and made myself a handle on the back.

I stood proudly in front of my mirror in my room and grinned. I was Captain America holding up the shield that would protect me from all the evildoers in the world.

Fast forward to 2005. I was working on the script for my play "The Homecoming Tree". It is the story of a group of people living in a boarding house in Shreveport, Louisiana at the beginning of World War II. The main character was a thirteen-year-old boy who was fascinated with beating the Nazis. I had interviewed my parents and my late brother extensively in the preceding few years about life in 1941. When I asked my brother who his heroes where he said, "The Shadow, Captain Midnight, and, of course, Captain America."

Captain America? In 1942? I did some research. As anyone who has seen the movie is aware, Captain America had his start as a comic book during World War II. It was shocking to realize that my brother and I had shared this connection I was never aware of. He passed away in 2008 but he had the opportunity to see "The Homecoming Tree". My mother passed away in 2004, but not only did my father get to see the play, he sang "There's a Star Spangled Banner Hanging Somewhere", a 1941 song that I recorded and played as part of our radio music playing the background during the play.

I gave my main character a love for Captain America. I had the actor playing the young boy to make his own uniform. Guess what he did? He found an old serving tray made out of plastic very similar to my tray and put the star and the stripes on it. Only, he didn't make the lines perfect as I did. He even found some old red gloves and when he came out onto the stage the first night of performance as "Captain America" I was back in my front yard wrapped in heat and humidity, shield up to ward off the bullets of my enemies, sweat soaking my blue tee shirt as I fought off the evil drones of death and destruction.

So, this weekend, I cannot wait to see "The Avengers". The original Avengers were my heroes way back in the 1960's when I discovered comic books and I cannot wait to hear those words: "Avengers Assemble!" and see Captain America once again stand up for what is right! I'll see you there!

(Note: Avengers Assemble was never uttered until the final movie in the Avengers cycle, Avengers: Endgame. It was uttered by Captain America and I stood up in the theater and cheered!)

CHAPTER 18

FOR RONALD ENNIS, MY NEPHEW AT CHRISTMAS (2012)

Mortality versus morbidity.

Strange words unless you are in the health care field.

Morbidity is the bad things that happen during a disease.

Mortality is death, pure and simple.

Some diseases have high morbidity but low mortality. They have really bad symptoms but you can get over them. Some diseases have low morbidity and high mortality because you die so quickly, you don't suffer.

A few years ago my nephew, Ronald Ennis, M.D. died suddenly at the age of 48. He was a pathologist in Dennison, Texas and was well respected and well loved by his friends and family. Ronald is one of those rare success stories of children who have a difficult childhood but rise above it. Ronald was one of the kindest people I have ever known. Even though he lived hours away in Dennison, Texas every Christmas he would come to see my mother and daddy and bring them a fruit basket. He loved my mother and father.

I'm not sure what happened to Ronald. His father's family

history is rife with early deaths in the fifties of his uncles from heart disease. And, his father has had heart disease. So, it seems he took a shower and was getting ready for work and just dropped dead. His wife and daughter found him. This is never a good thing for any wife or child to remember. But I will recall and remember Ronald fondly as one of the nicest, most motivated, hardest working people I ever knew.

That is why this past Tuesday while walking in the heat I felt the call of mortality. No morbidity, just mortality. I started having chest pains during my walk and they were not getting any easier. I've never had such pains and I stopped to ask a yard man if I could use his cell phone. Within 45 minutes, I was in the ER with a dozen or so health care personnel swarming over me. I knew I had already beaten the odds. Most massive heart attacks never survive the first thirty minutes. My chest pain was getting better on its own before I ever got the first shot of morphine. But, quite a bit of thinking occurred during those hours.

Have I really done for God what I should do? For, I believe with all my heart and mind and soul that only work done for God that has eternal consequences and that touches people is worth your time and effort. All else will fade.

Do my friends and family know I love them? I'll never forget taking my kids to Sears when they were preteens and having the check-out lady ask them if I had told them "I love you" today. I was proud when both of them said yes. For, that is something I say to my kids every time we talk. "I love you" can be the hardest words to utter and yet the most powerful.

What will be my legacy? We all wonder if we will be remembered. I was in the middle of finishing up a major rewrite on my fourth book. I left the manuscript open and unsaved when I went for a walk. What would happen if I did not return to finish it? Would anyone know what I was trying to say in my book? Would anyone care? I realized that the most important legacy I can leave is to know that I responded to God's invitation to join Him in His work, not MY work. I learned a hard lesson when I went through my depression and my daily prayer is that I do what God wills for me to do today! I hope that is what people will remember about Bruce Hennigan. I know my books will never be "literature" and will never be required reading. But, through my writing, God has used me to touch people's lives and has used those words to change people.

Am I about to die? As I was placed on the cardiac catheterization table, I was crying. I am a physician. I know all too well every conceivable outcome and consequence. I know the morbidity and the mortality! I prayed a simple prayer. "God give me the courage to face this with the faith and knowledge that Your will is done whether I wake up after the procedure; wake up after surgery; or wake up in heaven." And, as the nurse was giving me my Versed, I knew that I would remember nothing of the subsequent test and would awaken an hour or two later hopefully in my hospital room with good news.

As the Versed kicked in, nothing happened. Nothing. My memory did not fade. I recalled everything that happened. I remember my cardiologist telling me each step of the procedure and I felt the contrast in my aorta and in my coronaries. I recalled him saying everything was normal. I recall him asking me if I wanted to have pressure applied to my groin puncture or an angioseal (a plug that does not require holding pressure to stop the bleeding) and how painful it was when he put in the angioseal. I recall him squatting down so he could look me in the eye and tell me my test was normal and he was going to go tell my wife. I did not have to wake up. I was awake and, frankly, grateful for it. For, I heard and saw the professionalism and care of the team that took care of me.

That evening, as my wife was taking us home from the hospital, I marveled at how good God is. I had faced my own mortality and found that everything about my heart was stone cold normal. But, why hadn't that been true for my nephew? Why hadn't he had the chance I had? I cannot know God's will and I cannot know God's plans. But, this one thing I do know. I must make every moment; every opportunity count for God. He has given me more time and that is the one precious gift we can give back to Him.

Morbidity 1.

Mortality 0.

If you are planning a gift to the American Heart Association, give in memory of Ronald Ennis, M.D. He was a good man!

CHAPTER 19

SWINGIN' ON A STAR
A Christmas Tribute to my favorite author, Ray Bradbury

The wind whispered secrets down the cold, dark alleyway and Tasha listened. The secrets came from the lips of angels.

"LISTEN, Suzie, cain't you hear the angels talking?" Tasha whispered.

SUZIE PULLED her little sister closer to her. "Ain't no angels, Tash. Ain't no angels anywhere in this world. Only devils. We got to get out of here."

. . .

A BITE OF SOMETHING SWEET

Tasha wiped her runny nose and glanced back down the alleyway. Mist swirled around the trash containers and pulsed with the red and green of exit signs. "But, they gonna tell us how to get home. We lost, ain't we?"

Suzie stopped at the opening to the city street and her eyes were drawn to the huddled figures moving monotonously down the neon splashed sidewalks. Grizzled faces with tinted eyes bore down on them. "If we can just find the subway, we be all right."

The tinkle of metal and glass echoed from behind them. Tasha hugged her older sister's leg. "The angels done gone, Suzie. They ain't behind us no more. I'm scared."
Suzie glanced over her shoulder at the menacing maw of the alleyway. Its dim eyes glowed in the mist and its jaws paused to close. She stepped out onto the open street into the arms of perdition.

The man jostled them and his smell encircled them in warm, redolent odor. His toothless grin shown through a cloud of gagging mist. Suzie pulled away from him with her hand gripped on Tasha's. They ran. They bumped down the street from body to body, bouncing against the grim reminders of humanity caught between divinity and condemnation.

Suzie pulled them into an alcove. A dirty glass window was behind them plastered with obscenities.

. . .

"What we gonna do, Suzie?" Tasha sniffled.

"We ain't going back, that's for sure. Toby gonna sell us for drugs."

"I miss Momma."

Suzie pulled the tiny face against her stained overcoat. "Me, too, Tash. Momma up with the angels."

Tasha's face lit up. "If we listen to the angels, maybe Momma can tell us where to go."

Suzie frowned. "Maybe so, Tash. But, we ain't going back to Toby. We don't even know if he our daddy."

Tasha pulled her knit cap up to expose her ears and glanced skyward. "Maybe we ain't listenin' hard enough."

Suzie's eyes drifted upward, above the misted detritus of humanity shuffling down the street, above the crumbling bricks and mortar of a dream gone bad to the clear, star filled night. The space station arced in perfect serenity. She remembered the dead dreams of a tiny, idealistic girl, eyes drawn to the possibilities of worlds virgin with pristine future. Dreams that had died in a crack haze of insanity and evil.

. . .

"I THINK those angels done got tired of listening to us humans. We done worn out our welcome."

"TASHA! SUZIE!" A hoarse voice echoed down the street.

SUZIE'S HEART raced and she pulled Tasha to her. "Toby!"

THEY PULLED BACK into the darkness of the alcove. Her feet were paralyzed with fear and suddenly the promising stars were eclipsed by chipped paint, crumbling brick, and misty haze. A hulking figure shadowed the sidewalk and Toby stepped out of the mist. His yellow eyes glowed with drug fever as he scanned the streets until they fell on the girls.

"THERE YOU HEATHENS ARE. Why you run away from Toby?" He leaned forward and his rancid breath filled the alcove. "I got some candy for you." His hands were behind his back.

TASHA LOOKED UP AT SUZIE. "We don't want none of your candy."

"LEAVE US ALONE, Toby. We don't need you no more."

TOBY'S GRIN faded to a leer of insane resolution. "Then you won't be needing this candy." His hands came out and Suzie saw the glint of light on metal. A gun and a pair of handcuffs. "Now let's put on these bracelets, little girls. I got some friends want to meet you."

LIGHT CRACKED SOMEWHERE inside Suzie's mind; star light, hope light, angel light and through the cloying mist she watched a star move across the cityscape, promising hope and redemption. She kicked out viciously and drove into her foot all the anger and desperation of a world that had lost its promise, lost its heart. Toby collapsed in sudden pain and writhed on the ground. Suzie jerked Tasha behind her and they ran over Toby's writhing body out into the mist.

"WE GOT TO RUN, Tash. We got to run and never stop."

TASHA CLAMBERED after her as her eyes misted with tears. "But I can't hear the angels, Suzie. We gotta stop and listen."

"WE AIN'T STOPPING, Tash. We ain't never gonna stop."

FIGURES BEGAN to materialize out of the mist, down the street, across the street. Somewhere behind them, Toby's angry cursing bounced from brick walls. Tash stumbled and Suzie lost her. The tiny girl disappeared into the mist. She slid to a stop and ran back along a chain link fence. No Tasha. Toby was coming. A gap in the chain link fence appeared from the mist. A tiny shred of fabric from Tasha's coat was caught on the rusted metal. Suzie squeezed through the gap and pulled it back together. Furiously she knitted the rusted, twisted metal edges together. She backed away into the mist and prayed that Tasha was somewhere within the fence. Toby's hulking figure rocketed by them, mist swirling behind him. She held her breath. Toby didn't come back.

SUZIE STOOD SUSPENDED in the low lying haze with her breath coming quickly and her heart racing. She calmed and paused to listen. To listen for an angel. A creaking sounded somewhere behind her. She stepped out of the mist into a clearing. A playground surrounded her. It was long abandoned filled with rusted metal frameworks like skeletons of dead beasts, dead hopes.

"TASHA." She whispered loudly. The creaking continued. Tasha sat in an old swing with her head bobbing down and then up. "Tasha, what are you doing?"

TASHA TURNED her face and her eyes bright with hope. "The angels, Suzie. They told me to reach up." The words waxed and waned as Tasha swung up and back. "See that star. See it way up there."

SUZIE SQUINTED in the darkness and spied a bright, pulsing star halfway up the horizon hovering above the misty horror of this world. "They say if I can touch it with my foot, if I can swing high enough, I can go there. Momma's there. She's an angel and she's helping them learn about God and goodness and all. They want us to go there, too."

. . .

SUZIE MOANED in sorrow and collapsed on the ground. Tasha moved higher and higher. "Tasha, that ain't gonna happen. Momma ain't no angel. She ain't on no planet in the sky. She dead. And, so are we. We can't go on running."

TASHA SEEMED NOT TO HEAR, stretching her foot farther out on each upward swing. "I almost got it, Suzie. I almost touched it. Come on, you gotta go, too. Momma's waiting. All you gotta do is try. Don't give up hope now."

SUZIE FELT the tears begin and the dam broke on months of hidden sorrow. Her heart fell as the cadence of the creaking swing increased. "There ain't no hope, no more, Tash. There ain't no angels."

LIGHT GUSHED AROUND HER, brighter than noonday sun, burning away the mist in a sudden gulp of warm air. A giggle echoed in the air and darkness returned. The swing tumbled down and was empty and stilled.

SUZIE RUSHED to the empty swing. "Tash? Tash?" Her eyes darted around the playground. It was empty and barren. She blinked away the burning aftermath of light as her heart raced.

"No! Don't leave me, too. Tasha, don't leave me!" Tears clouded her vision. Behind her, out in the desperate street she heard metal screech. Toby had found her. She glanced up at the star pulsing with hope and promise in the night; the star holding out the welcoming hand of a future and a hope. She climbed into the swing.

CHAPTER 20

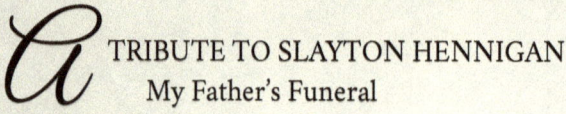 TRIBUTE TO SLAYTON HENNIGAN
My Father's Funeral

MY FATHER WAS a unique man who loved life and loved attention and loved the stage. He spent all of my life singing as a bi-vocational music minister. He was joined on many occasions by my mother and her strong alto. I grew up listening to music and singing along with my parents.

WHEN MY FATHER moved from assisted living to the nursing home end of "The Oaks of Louisiana" he was 95 and he was worried he would fade away; lose his identity. He was so afraid no one would know him. Well, he was so wrong. For, my father up until the week he died sang constantly for the workers and occupants of his wing of the nursing home. Just a year ago, he won first prize in a talent show at the assisted living end of his location for dressing as a woman and singing with three other men dressed as women. You see, my father would do just about anything in order to have the opportunity to sing!

IN FACT, he sang at his own funeral and anyone who knew Slayton Hennigan would have nodded and known instantly this was typical for him. So, I want to share with you a wonderful presentation from our Associate Pastor and Minister of Senior Adults at Brookwood Baptist Church, John Harp. John asked me for my father's Bible. But, my father, unlike my mother, did not write in his Bible. But, he had a box of sheet music he had collected over his entire lifetime. I gave the box of music to John and this is what he came up with. It was wonderful and exhilarating and a fantastic testimony to my father's life. I hope you enjoy it:

Funeral Service for DANIEL SLAYTON HENNIGAN
October 15, 2012 2:00 PM
PRELUDE
MINISTER 1 – Rev. Gary Palmer
Segue' – Thank you Gary. Slayton loved music. He loved to sing ... especially songs of faith. He took advantage of many family gatherings to demonstrate this by singing the song, *"There is Coming a Day"*. Sit back and enjoy this recording of Slayton and join me in looking forward to the happy day of reunion with our loved ones in eternity.

SONG – "THERE IS COMING A DAY" – CD (recorded by my father to be played at his own funeral.)

MINISTER 2 – Rev. John Harp
There is indeed coming a day when the downside of loving

and grief will be past-tense. Until then, we consider it worth the price to embrace our families and friends and let the warmth of life together keep us steady in a fulfilling life together.

SLAYTON WAS BORN JUNE 13, 1914 in Saline, LA to William and Lillie Hennigan. He professed his faith in Jesus Christ at the age of 11. He married Lena on July 27, 1935. She was 16 and he was 21. He told me on 07/27/04 that when he first saw Lena he said to himself, "***She has all the right stuff in all the right places.***" They enjoyed 69 years as husband and wife, ending only at her home-going on August 4, 2004.

SLAYTON WAS a Postal office worker until his retirement. He demonstrated his passion for music and worship by leading music in churches for 38 years. He lived in Blanchard for many of those years and led music at the First Baptist Church of Blanchard.

HE PLAYED the guitar and loved watching the ***Grand 'Ole Opry***. He truly had an entertainer's blood flowing through his veins. He enjoyed fishing and cooked the best fish on the Coleman propane Camp-stove.

SLAYTON WAS A "HANDY-MAN" too. He excelled in "rigging!" He was of the school that thought duct-tape could fix anything. He practiced his skill with his own flair. Every bathroom faucet he changed out gave HOT water through the handle marked "C" and COLD water through the one marked "H"!

. . .

I BECAME Associate Pastor at Brookwood 12 years ago, and seven years ago Slayton joined me in making several hospital visits. I was inspired because he then was 91 and still interested in serving God in some way. That impressed me.

YOU SAID it well when you wrote, "*Mr. Hennigan was a devoted husband, daddy, papaw, Great-grandpaw, and great-great-grandpaw. He loved to sing and entertain family and friends.*"

I mentioned Slayton's love for music a moment ago. He had song after song after song copied for use. However, not all of his singing was songs of faith. He had some interesting titles like ...

- "Blue Yodel No.6"
- "Blue Yodel No.7"
- "Blue Yodel No.8"
- "Blue Yodel No.9"
- "Blue Yodel No.10"
- "Blue Yodel No.11"
- "The Bull-Dog on The Bank"

HIS MUSIC DOES TELL much of his life. The clear majority of his music was songs that told a story ... the story of faith. Slayton's faith story began much the way ours does, with an awareness of God reaching into our world through His Son, Jesus Christ. How many times did we hear him burst forth in song, "**O Holy Night**"?

. . .

From the Bethlehem birthplace, Slayton, at age 11, journeyed and knelt at the foot of Jesus' cross and pledged his faith in Christ Jesus as Lord and Savior. That was a day he never forgot and gave direction for his life's journey, one of love and praise to his Savior. We heard the passion in his voice as he sang, "**A Hill Called Mount Calvary**," a song that heralded his statement of Faith.

From that day forward, Slayton's life had a theme. The love he had for you and me, was firm because its foundation was a righteous love for his Savior. With all the beauties of the world, he kept balance in an upright perspective. "**I'd Rather Have Jesus**" he clearly marked in another song book. We can say of him that *he kept choosing Jesus* through his whole life.

Just as he kept choosing Jesus, he chose to keep "**Standing on the Promises**" of God (#335) for daily living. God spoke truths in His Word, and Slayton believed them and lived in their benefit. As a result, his affection for Jesus continued to grow. It is no wonder that he prized the hymns "**Just a Closer Walk with Thee**" (#448) and "**I Need Thee Every Hour**" (#450).

Lest you think that the Christian life is just a humble dependency on our Lord, you must realize that is simply the foundation from which the believer in Christ is able to have joy beyond the circumstances and see the glory beyond the grief. Slayton embraced this truth and shared it strongly when he belted out the hymn, "**Because He Lives**"! Looking forward in such a way guided the path for a sweet, deep joy in service to God for the good of others around him. The joy seemed to deepen with maturity. As years evolved into decades, Slayton found truth in the hymn, "**The Longer I Serve Him the Sweeter He Grows.**"

As the years progressed, so did the genre' of the musical theme. With feet firmly planted in this world, his heart began to dwell more on his future hope of heaven. Several hymns began to carry a deeper meaning and growing affection. Hymns like "**Mansion Over the Hilltop**", "**I'll Fly Away**", and "**The Holy City**".

Witnessing first hand this glorious anticipation Slayton owned, I understand better why he chose as special the hymn of question, "**How Long Has It Been?**"

How long has it been since you talked with the Lord
And told him your heart's hidden secrets
How long since you prayed how long since you stayed
On your knees till the light shone through
How long has it been since your mind felt at ease
How long since your heart knew no burden
Can you call him your friend how long has it been since you knew
that he cared for you?

Surely that is the question for us today. Do you know that Jesus cares for you? Do you know that he gave his life to give you a chance to receive eternal life? Do you know that He cares for you? If you don't you can discover God's love today.
  "**In Times Like These**"

. . .

IF YOU DO KNOW God's great love for you then you can join Slayton and all the redeemed in some of the great songs of hope that celebrate God's great love for us and His eternal home for us.

Songs like ... "**How Great Thou Art**" and "**I'll Meet You in the Morning**". But I think my favorite for Slayton is "**Where We'll Never Grow Old**" because at 98 he can say, *"Been there; done that!"*

I WANT to leave you with God's Word from Philippians 4.8-9. Paul writes these encouraging words from his heart to ours ... *"Finally, whatever is true, whatever is noble, whatever is right, whatever is pure, whatever is lovely, whatever is admirable—if anything is excellent or praiseworthy—think about these things. Whatever you have learned or received or heard from me, or seen in me—put it into practice. And the God of peace will be with you."*

Indeed, may God's peace be on you all!
CLOSE W/PRAYER

CHAPTER 21

We All Gotta Thank Someone (2012)

There was an empty chair at the table this Thanksgiving.

My father passed away a few weeks ago at the age of 98. Even though he had been living in the nursing home for the past three years, I always brought him home for the holidays. Every Thanksgiving, Christmas, and Fourth of July, my father would sit at the head of our table. And, always, he would lead us in prayer and sing us a song or two.

My father's singing idols were Tennessee Ernie Ford and George Beverly Shea. Although his voice was weaker and weaker as he aged, when he switched to his singing mode, from somewhere deep within, this clear, deep, resonant voice would boom out a song in perfect pitch.

And so, this year, more than any other, I am thankful for my father. His absence has made me realize how much I came to depend on hearing that voice raised in song. My father was also a story teller and he used his imagination to infuse his tales with power.

I inherited that imagination. One dark day atop a tall tree I realized the world was broken and no longer the glowing, innocent thing I had lived in for my first ten years. It was atop that tree, above the vampires that lurked in the dark shadows and the werewolves with glowing yellow eyes that waited for me in the blackberry bushes and the myriad monsters of my imagination that my fear of the worlds I had only until then imagined, became the beasts of approaching adulthood. Just as real. Just as dangerous. Just as deadly.

I WRITE about vampires and werewolves and creatures in the dark because we live in a broken, fallen world. We try desperately to understand it and to dissect it and to equate it and to reduce it to laws and axioms that fit neatly into a science textbook. Equations we can control. With them we hope to tame the beasts but to no avail. Rather, it takes imagination.

DURING A MIDNIGHT WALK, J. R. R. Tolkien told C. S. Lewis that his atheism was no more than a lack of imagination.

I AM SO thankful for the power of my imagination to open up the doorways of my heart and mind to the REALITY of God! I am so thankful my God standing in the gap between my soul and the monsters of my brokenness is real and loving and forgiving and the author and finisher of this universe. I am so thankful for the times of failure and faithlessness and doubt so that I could search those shadows again and find Him waiting there right where I left Him. I am so thankful my father showed me the love of God! I am thankful for each and every reader that has trusted me to fill a book with words that are more than echoes of futility. Rather, they are words that lead slowly but inexorably to the Word, the Logos, the One who became flesh. And, for that, I am thankful.

LOOK around you in the aftermath of this hectic and busy season of empty thanks and muted praise and awkward family gatherings and frantic hours of shopping. Stop and look into the shadows. There may be beasts among us, and I am sure there are. But there is a quiet, abiding Companion following, following and watching over us. My father sang of this Companion in his powerful voice. He sang of a Father that is greater than any earthly father could ever be. A Father who sits at our table; who sings the story of our lives into being; who longs to love us and redeem us and hold us in his arms. Think on this with an imagination that is a poor reflection of the image of God and you will find in your heart and in your soul the need to thank Someone!

CHAPTER 22

WE'LL FOLLOW THE OLD MAN

EVERY CHRISTMAS I make sure and watch one of my favorite movies of all time, White Christmas. Yes, I love the song. Yes, I love the romantic angle. Yes, I love the story of loyalty to old friends. But the real reason this movie touches me is because of the relationship between General Waverly and his men. When the film opens, a tired, war weary group of men are trying to celebrate Christmas Eve on the German front. General Waverly is being sent back to the states. The men sing a song to "the old man".

> WE'LL FOLLOW *the old man wherever he wants to go*
>   *Long as he wants to go opposite to the foe*
>   *We'll stay with the old man wherever he wants to stay*
>   *Long as he stays away from the battle's fray*
>   *Because we love him, we love him*

*Especially when he keeps us on the ball
And we'll tell the kiddies we answered duty's call
With the grandest son of a soldier of them all!*

IT IS hard for us to understand this kind of devotion in today's jaded, cynical world. A group of men so tightly devoted to each other they would tell their leader they "love" him? Unthinkable!

Why did they love General Waverly so? What characteristics of his leadership inspired this kind of devotion? A key to understanding the answer to this question can be found in the following dialogue. Bob Wallace, played by Bing Crosby and Phil Davis, played by Danny Kaye have arrived at the General's inn in Vermont and watch as the man once a commander is now cleaning kitchen floors. This is what they said:

BOB WALLACE: We ate, and then he ate. We slept, then he slept.

PHIL DAVIS: Yeah, then he woke up and nobody slept for forty-eight hours.

ONE OF MY favorite photographs shows Walt Disney walking through Snow White's castle in a very early Disneyland. Walt was famous for his "management by walking around" philosophy. He would pop up unannounced and ride the rides; watch the shows; listen to the musicians. Yes, he was a stickler for quality but more than anything, he wanted to be a part of his creation. He would wander the hallways of the animation studio after the animators left for the day and dig through their trash to find new ideas. He really believed in his animators. And, his expectations were very tight and rigid, but inside he cared about his employees; he loved them. There were many times he would take an employee who was in trouble and pay his salary while he dried out in what we would call today "rehab". In fact, when his animators joined the union, Walt was devastated. He considered them a part of his family and the decision to join the union was akin to saying they didn't appreciate his tender care.

MANY BOOKS HAVE BEEN WRITTEN about Jesus' "leadership" style but I believe it comes down to a simple act that typified Jesus' approach to assuring these men would indeed change the world.

It is the night of his betrayal and Jesus and his disciples are gathered in a room to celebrate the feast of unleavened bread prior to the Passover. It is a somber and moving dinner filled with meaning and remembrance of the passing over the children of Israel by the angel of death while they were slaves in Eqypt. Imagine the men talking among themselves; eager to take their place at the right hand of this new king who would soon overthrow the tyranny of the Romans. They are excited; filled with hubris and arrogance; over confident after Jesus' reception by the people of Jerusalem. Suddenly, the door to the other room opens. Standing in the doorway is Jesus. He has taken off his robe and wrapped a towel around his bare waist. His chest glistens with sweat and his eyes are filled with a haunting passion. He holds a wooden bowl filled with tepid water. As the disciples watch in utter amazement, this man; this king; this ruler of all of mankind kneels before the first of his disciples and begins to wash the man's nasty, dirty feet.

SHOCKED AND STUNNED they whisper among themselves as their leader takes their feet, dipping them into the warm water and washes away the dirt. Their king is kneeling before THEM! The world has turned upside down.

THIS STUNNING DEVELOPMENT was just the beginning of a huge paradigm shift for these men. Later, anticipating a board room meeting in which each man would receive his marching orders and his assignment in the new hierarchy Jesus shocks them again with these words:

"AS THE FATHER has loved me, so have I loved you. Now remain in my love. If you keep my commands, you will remain in my love, just as I have kept my Father's commands and remain in his love. I have told you this so that my joy may be in you and that your joy may be complete. My command is this: Love each other as I have loved you.

STOP HERE for a moment and really hear those words. Jesus is talking about love? Not conquest or battle strategy or corporate intrigue. He has become a servant to his men and now he speaks of love! How has he loved these men? Listen to his next words:

GREATER LOVE HAS no one than this: to lay down one's life for one's friends. You are my friends if you do what I command. I no longer call you servants, because a servant does not know his master's business. Instead, I have called you friends, for everything that I learned from my Father I have made known to you. You did not choose me, but I chose you and appointed you so that you might go and bear fruit—fruit that will last—and so that whatever you ask in my name the Father will give you. This is my command: Love each other.

. . .

THERE IS an awful lot love mentioned in this section. The word here is a Greek word, agape meaning "the love of God or Christ for humankind. In the New Testament, it refers to the covenant love of God for humans, as well as the human reciprocal love for God; the term necessarily extends to the love of one's fellow man. Many have thought that this word represents divine, unconditional, self-sacrificing, active, volitional, and thoughtful love."

IN FACT, the original Greek word, *agapao*, has taken on this meaning through its use by Jesus of Nazareth and his followers. There are some interesting words in the above definition such as "the love of one's fellow man" and "unconditional, self-sacrificing". I could go on but let's stop right here for now. Let's look at what Jesus of Nazareth is telling us about his concept of being a "king" or a "leader". Simply, put Jesus of Nazareth is teaching us:

YOU CANNOT BE an effective leader until you know how to follow.
You cannot ask someone to serve you until you know what it is like to serve someone.
Loyalty is freely given and cannot be demanded.
The truest form of "friendship" is based on "agape" love.
Jesus of Nazareth redefined love as unconditional and self-sacrificial love for his fellow man; his friends.

AS THIS SEASON APPROACHES, no matter what your worldview; no matter if you believe in God or not; these simple teachings of

Jesus of Nazareth carry profound implications for us today. If we are to be the kind of leader that changes the world; the kind of leader that results in "love" from our "followers"; the kind of leader that inspires the kind of creativity and self-sacrifice we see in the above two modern examples then we must first understand that the highest place to lead from is often at the feet of those we serve!

CHAPTER 23

I WAS WONDERING
For Sue

W*HY IS* a round pizza put in a square box?

Can you cry under the water?

Is it still called a hearing when a deaf person goes to court?

If you have a cured ham, what disease did it have?

Will you be fired if you drink Pepsi at a Coke factory?

Does a person have to be important before they are considered assassinated instead of just plain murdered?

If sandwich bread is square, then why are most luncheon meats round?

When you go to Heaven, do you wear the clothes you were buried in forever?

Babies wake up almost every two hours or so, then why do we say, "I slept like a baby"?

Why did man walk on the moon before it was discovered that wheels could be put on luggage?

Why go to the top of a tall building only to put money in binoculars to look at things on the ground?

Money does not grow on trees then why do banks have branches?

Why do you "put your two cents in" when it is only "a penny for your thoughts"? What happens to the other penny?

If you are IN a movie, why are you ON TV?

Once you've heard a sound, where does the sound go?

What color is a chameleon?

In a light tight room from where light cannot escape, when you turn off the light bulb, where does the light that filled the room go?

Why is it called the Afterlife when it's really Afterdeath?

Why is it called after dark when it's really Afterlight?

What was the best thing before sliced bread?

Why do 24/7 stores have locks fitted to the doors?

Why are soapsuds always white?

Why do Superheroes wear tights?

If Buzz Lightyear doesn't know he's a toy, why does he stop talking when humans are around?

If humans left the earth, would time cease to exist?

Why do psychics keep sending me spam? Don't they know I'm not interested?

What was the root of all evil before money?

If we all stopped voting, would the politicians go away?

What seeds were used for seedless grapes?

Why do kids always make the wrong comment at the wrong time in front of the wrong people?

Why are there no size "B" batteries ?

Why are they called a**part**ments when they are units "all together"?

Why is an army called an **infant**ry if you have to be over 18 to get in?

Isn't it scary that a doctor's office is called a practice?

Why can't you tickle yourself (but others can)?

Why are carrots not called oranges, as they are more orange than oranges?

Why are builders afraid of a 13th floor, but publishers not afraid of a chapter 11?

If a seagull flew over the bay, would it be called a bagel?

Do pediatricians play miniature golf?

What is the speed of dark?

Did the early settlers go camping?

Can race car drivers deduct speeding tickets?

If a fly didn't have wings, would it be called a walk?

How much wood can a woodchuck chuck?

Can an ambidextrous person make an offhand remark?

Do you feed a boogie fever?

If you're born again, do you have two bellybuttons?

Why don't they invent a cordless extension cord?

Why is it when driving and looking for an address, we turn down the radio?

Why do people ask if you remember where they were when someone famous was killed? (Do they have to prove an alibi?)

Does condensed milk comes from smaller cows?

If a turtle loses its shell, is it considered naked or homeless?

Why did the chicken really cross the road?

Why does an alarm clock go off, by going on?

If a vampire cannot see its reflection, how is their hair always so neat?

Why is cheese so secret that we must shred it?

When a cow laughs, does milk come out its nose?

What do they use to ship Styrofoam?

Why do we wait until a pig is dead to cure it?

Do infants enjoy infancy as much as adults enjoy adultery?

Can you tell how old a pirate is by cutting off his peg leg and counting the rings?

Do Scottish Terriers get Scotch tapeworms?
Does the person who inventories sheep often fall asleep on the job?
What is another word for thesaurus?
Why do we put suits in a garment bag and put garments in a suitcase?
If a person thinks marathons are superior to sprints, is that racism?
Can fat people go skinny dipping?
How do you let someone know you painted a wet paint sign?
Is it possible to have a civil war?
Why do they call it a TV set, when there is only one?
What happens if you get scared 1/2 to death twice?
Before they invented drawing boards, what did they go back to?
If "Con" is the opposite of "Pro," is Congress opposed to progress?
Is animal shampoo tested on humans?
Why don't they call moustaches mouthbrows?
Could it be that boulders are statues of big rocks?
Can they put more clowns than people in a taxi?
If the #2 pencil is the most popular, why is it still #2?
Do fish get thirsty?
Why is abbreviation such a long word?
How would you throw away a garbage can?
Do vegetarians eat animal crackers?
Do bleach blondes pretend to have more fun?
Why is it when you transport something by car it's called a shipment,
but when you transport something by ship it's called cargo?
Why isn't the word phonetic spelled like it sounds?
Do police sketch artists start out by drawing chalk outlines?
Why don't they just make food stamps edible?
Would they invent fireproof matches?

Would they invent a solar powered flashlight?

After eating, do amphibians have to wait one hour before getting OUT of the water?

When it rains, do cotton fields shrink?

Do chickens think rubber humans are funny?

Why do we park on a driveway and drive on a parkway?

CHAPTER 24

*G*UILT IN THE MOUNTAINS:
CHRISTMAS IN JULY

Growing up in the wooded pastures and flat lands of Louisiana, as a child I dreamed of one day climbing a mountain. The highest point in Louisiana is less than 200 feet above sea level, Mount Driskill. And so it was when at the age of 10 my father loaded up the family to journey west, I realized I would see my dream fulfilled.

There were seven of us in a bucket seat, two door Impala. My father and mother sat in the front. My sister Gwen and her husband sat in the back. My place was either sitting with my legs on either side of the stick shift or lying flat in the back window of the car, looking up through the rear window at the sky. My two nephews, Keith and Kevin were younger and smaller and fit in the center seat between the two back passengers. We pulled a pop-up tent housed in a small trailer that slept four adults. The three of us kids were tucked into cubby holes or spread out on the floor whenever the tent was deployed.

We started out in Shreveport, Louisiana and journeyed across Texas, New Mexico, Arizona, northward through Utah, into Wyoming, southward through Colorado and back into Texas and then home. Ten days we traveled like sardines packed in a can on wheels. Somewhere in Arizona, I begged my father to stop so I could please climb a mountain. We pulled off on the side of the road in the middle of a desert landscape while I scrambled up a hill that was, in truth, not as high as Mount Driskill. But, in my childish mind it was a REAL mountain!

In mid-July, our car broke down along a highway outside of Logan, Utah. In our naïveté, we had packed tee shirts and shorts. But, here in the mountains, it was cold and snowing. Yes, snowing in mid-July! I was delighted even as my teeth chattered, and my lips turned blue sitting in the snow covered car waiting for someone to give my father or my brother-in-law a ride into town. But, no one stopped and the hours passed. The air grew colder. My father had on a small sweater and he and my brother-in-law set out walking toward the nearest town.

An hour later, a van pulled up and my father hopped out. An elderly couple had picked them up. We loaded into the van and the couple took us to their home on the side of a mountain. It was an A-frame house unlike anything I had ever seen in Louisiana. To my mind, it was futuristic and awe inspiring. The living room was open all the way up to the peaked roof. A balcony in the back part of the house looked down on the living room. They had one of those James Bond type fireplaces that looked like an inverted funnel! And, just outside the back porch, was the mountain side! Keith and I gazed up in amazement at the sloping mountainside covered with rocks and trees. It was growing late in the evening and the couple had agreed to let us spend the night while our car was being repaired in Logan.

While they cooked a most fragrant dinner, Keith and I did what I had always wanted to do. We climbed a real mountain. I labored up the sharp slope, my chest aching with the thin air. But I was in heaven! Far above us, the peak beckoned but we soon realized we could never make it before night fall. Best to stop now and maybe we could try again in the morning. It was then we found the boulder. I would say it was maybe four feet in diameter, lodged against a tall tree. Or, rather, the tree had grown from under it.

I instantly replayed scenes from my favorite science fiction shows. Huge aliens picking up boulders and tossing them like marshmallows. Or, boulders rolling down a hill to pick off the bad guy right before he pulled the trigger on his ray gun. Keith must have read my mind for we shoved against that boulder and dislodged it from the tree. It pivoted ever so slowly and then began to roll down the hill. I watched in utter amazement as it mowed down small bushes and bounced over smaller rocks and, yes, gained speed. Then, my heart was gripped with horror. It was headed right for the house! Faster and faster it rolled, now a mighty engine of destruction. It ramped a small fallen tree, gained some air and crashed through the back porch railing. Undeterred, it exploded through the rear sliding doors and finally came to rest in the kitchen where our hosts stood open mouthed and shocked.

In the aftermath of that tragedy, I allowed my parents and our hosts to assume the rock had dislodged under its own power as the soil on the mountain side had absorbed quite a bit of water from melting snow in the past few days. I never told anyone we were the source of the dislodging!

That guilt festered for months. And, even now, over fifty years later, it eats away at my insides. Confession is good for the soul, but my parents and, most assuredly that couple, have long since gone on to their eternal rewards and I never took the opportunity to confess. Those of us left behind live with that guilt. I share this because guilt is such a powerful motivator in our lives. But guilt can also eat away at us like a cancer. Like that boulder slowly tumbling down the mountainside, guilt can gain momentum and gather to itself other bits of guilt debris left over by other unconfessed deeds. Guilt lives all around us just as the mountain side is covered in rocks. And, all it takes is for us to bump against one of those hoarded guilts to start the avalanche of depression.

We completed the trip that summer. The couple that picked us up told us there had been a heinous murder the week before. A family had picked up a hitchhiker along that stretch of highway and he had murdered the entire family. He was never arrested. Because of this crime, car after car passed us by afraid for their very lives. And, I am sure that many of them felt guilty as they left us behind on the snowy road in the mountains.

You see, guilt begets guilt. It can become an endless cycle that builds and builds and affects so many more around us than just ourselves. But, every now and then, we recognize guilt for what it is and we stop and we do good and we do right in spite of the possible harm to ourselves. One elderly couple stopped and picked up two strangers on a snowy road and saved our lives. They didn't let guilt stop them from doing good. Don't let guilt paralyze you today. Move past it or it will barrel through the railings of your protection and crash into your life and leave you stranded on the road of depression! Get rid of the guilt of your past and make amends for those errors and wrongs you think you have done. Forgive and be forgiven. Get rid of the guilt and climb the mountain of depression where you can eventually step up into the sunshine and gaze out onto a marvelous world that God has made just for you!

CHAPTER 25

ORE FLOWERS FOR CHRISTMAS

My thanks to Micah, my Hutchmoot Secret Santa for an awesome book. "The Science Fiction Hall of Fame" really took me back to my teenage years. Many of the stories I recall reading way back then in other anthologies as "classic science fiction". It was a real treasure to read some of them again. My favorite so far, "Flowers for Algernon" by Daniel Keyes. This story of a mentally challenged man who is given an operation that triples his I.Q. only to lose it again was one of the most moving and touching stories I ever read. I just read it again and it is as moving and timeless today as when it was published in 1959.

Charlie's struggle with growing awareness of the world around him as his intelligence grew reminded me of my own growing awareness of the brokenness of the world around me as I aged. It is a story of the loss of innocence. Like Charlie, I cherished the laughter from other kids over my lack of co-ordination growing up. I even played to that clumsiness, capitalizing on it to gain recognition. When I was a junior in high school, I transformed this slapstick schtick into a dramatic role in a play.

Because of the popularity of that role, I won the election for student council president for my senior year.

After I felt a call to be a doctor, I was alarmed when my own mother began telling others that she didn't think I could be a doctor because I might "drop somebody's brain during surgery. He trips over his own feet." I realized I had become what others saw in me. I had fulfilled my own worst nightmare. We become what people see in us. How many times have we said "I will never be like that!" when seeing traits in our parents that are undesirable only to find ourselves shaking an angry finger at our own children and wondering "How did I get my father's finger?"

Charlie, in "Flowers of Algernon" has a moment when he sees a mentally challenged boy break dishes at a cafe. He watches in horror as people laugh and make fun of the boy and the boy smiles right back, unaware he is being ridiculed. For Charlie, the horror of that moment comes when he realizes he laughed, too!

In this time of year when we celebrate the birth of Jesus of Nazareth, we see both good and bad discussions of the Nativity. The "war on Christmas" always arises and the arguments are strident and shrill. The inevitable atheist attacks on Christianity reach their highest point such as the billboard in Times Square that says "Dump the Myth" with a picture of the crucified Jesus. And yet, they say there is "no agenda".

Every human being is born with an innate knowledge of God. Even science has discovered that the human brain is "hard wired" to believe in God. We have to teach our children to be atheists. Richard Dawkins has written a book in the last year aimed at children to tell them that belief in God is wrong and that believing in science and evolution is the elegant and beautiful thing to do. If there is no God, then why hasn't He disappeared from our collective consciousness over the past two thousand years? We have tried and tried to remove God from our thinking; from our culture; from our world. And yet, God keeps resurfacing; showing up over and over in spite of our efforts to move to a more civilized, non superstitious, evolved level.

Could it be that like the mentally challenged Charlie, we are unaware of the effect God has on our lives until we see Him clearly? Like the boy breaking the dishes, we keep having these moments of clarity and paradigm shifting when we see through our human veil the divine. In that moment, instead of laughing, some of us are horrified; alarmed; afraid of the existence of God. What does that mean for our lives? What will we become if we accept that there is a God? We will no longer be free to be our own god; to form our own morality; to answer only to our own needs. Science answers the "how" but cannot answer the "why". Science gave Charlie a huge increase in his intelligence but at the price of his innocence. Science might have made Charlie smart, but it was his experience with others that made Charlie wise. Ah, there is the rub. Science makes us smart. God makes us wise.

Charlie was not bitter when his mind returned once again to the state of shattered innocence. The one thing he recalled was true meaning of friendship and the significance of love. In order to spare his friends, the pain of seeing him in his fallen state, his love for them drove him to leave his work and his friends and find a new life.

In my final installment of the teachings of Jesus it is fitting that his most memorable sermon should be mentioned:

"Blessed are the poor in spirit, for theirs is the kingdom of heaven.

"Blessed are those who mourn, for they shall be comforted.

"Blessed are the meek, for they shall inherit the earth.

"Blessed are those who hunger and thirst for righteousness, for they shall be satisfied.

"Blessed are the merciful, for they shall receive mercy.

"Blessed are the pure in heart, for they shall see God.

"Blessed are the peacemakers, for they shall be called sons of God.

"Blessed are those who are persecuted for righteousness' sake, for theirs is the kingdom of heaven.

"Blessed are you when others revile you and persecute you and utter all kinds of evil against you falsely on my account. Rejoice and be glad, for your reward is great in heaven, for so they persecuted the prophets who were before you.

We are not blessed if we are simple minded like Charlie before his operation. We are blessed because we have seen God; we have come to know our fallen state. God's presence in our lives has shown us the emptiness of selfishness; of arrogance; of pride. I have been God and I did not like it at all. My mother's words about my incoordination were a cold wash of shame, but they served to remind me I am not perfect. And, only God can be perfect. I must look outside myself for God's standard and His love to find meaning for my life. As long as I go along within my own strength, being my own god, I will stumble and fall and fail and laugh and be laughed at. But humility, meekness, mercy, peace are the gifts of living against the standard of God and not in its place.

This holiday season, see those around you. Do not laugh; do not ridicule; do not be arrogant and prideful and godlike. Rather, see your own weaknesses and revel in them; rely on God to supplant those weaknesses with new strengths that will give you an eternal perspective on the world around you. And, then, put away the things of the past and place some flowers on the grave of Algernon. Move on in God's strength and make the coming years and all the years after that truly Blessed!

CHAPTER 26

TOO GOOD TO BE TRUE: LOST IN THE SNOW
If it's too good to be true . . .

A family friend contacted me the other day to take a look at an online video advertising a new product. This product was the results of a "scientific breakthrough" in genetics and promised to do something incredible. I won't disclose the actual claim because I don't want to, in any way, endorse the product. Suffice it to say the claim was something on the lines of "total reversal of the aging process". Turn back the clock. Be young again. What was interesting was that the advertisement never gave any indication what the actual product was. Was it a lotion? Was it a pill? Was it an injection? Was it a soaking bath? Was it a projector of alien anti-aging cosmic rays?

I spoke to my friend and my answer was very simple. If it seems too good to be true, then it IS too good to be true. Robert Heinlein, the famous science fiction writer once wrote "there is no such thing as a free lunch". Basically, there is always a catch. There is always an agenda. There is always a downside to every offer that seems too good to be true.

But, sometimes, it is not an offer. Sometimes, it is a possibility. I've had many of these in my life. A seeming "coincidence" that promised something that seemed unobtainable; something I was unworthy of. Sometimes, it seems to be a gift. From God. From a friend. From a stranger, even.

Years ago, I was wearing the new soft contact lenses. These new lenses (this was in the 1990's) could not be worn at night. And, they were far too expensive to be disposable. Each set of lenses was meant to last a couple of years. My wife and I left our children in the capable hands of their grandparents and we went snow skiing. The first night after our first day of skiing was, as usual, very painful. Muscles I had not been using were stressed by having to walk in those horrendous ski boots. Not to mention muscles strained by my desire to ski down the mountain as fast as possible, consequences be damned!

That evening, we found a hot tub and eased into the soaking, heated, wondrous embrace of those bubbles. There were at least six of us staying in the condo. Friends from ski trips in the past. Suddenly, a bubble burst near my face and I felt my contact lens slide off my cornea. I sat up quickly, leaned over the side of the hot tub so that my eye was above the snow covered deck. That way, if the lens popped out, it would NOT land in the caldron of hot tub bubbles. Alas, I did not move quickly enough and the lens was gone! Now what was I to do? I only had one pair of lenses. And, there was no way I could ski to my liking in my glasses.

A friend offered one of her contact lenses. Of course, it was too good to be true that it would work on me and it didn't. By the time I made it down the slopes the next day, my right eye was killing me. The lens offered by my friend was never meant for my eye. That night, we went back out to the hot tub to soak our even more painful muscles. My glasses clouded up but I had to wear them to see. My friend was upset I could not wear her extra set of lenses and another of our friends who had not been in the hot tub with us the night before asked me how I lost my lens. I recreated my movement and hung my head over the edge of the hot tub and there, nestled in a tiny pool of melted water in a crater of snow floated my contact lens! I gasped in amazement. My lens was right in front of me, still there from the night before! How could such a thing happen? It was too good to be true!

My conclusion is that every now and then, what is too good to be true is still true. Sometimes, good things happen in spite of the negativity that swirls around us. In fact, as I look back on my life, I can find many examples of good things that seemed to happen out of the blue. When these things happened, invariably it was an unexpected answer to a prayer. Or, it was an open door that eventually led me in a direction that proved beneficial in the long run -- a door that I never would have walked through on my own.

What I am saying is that sometimes Providence is too good to be true because in our human expectations, we cannot see the future from an eternal perspective. We only see the immediate. Meet my needs now! Give me what I want today!

In one of my favorite movies, White Christmas, Bing Crosby's character sings this chorus of a song to his true love:

If you're worried and you can't sleep,
just count your blessings instead of sheep
and you'll fall asleep counting your blessings.

This always gives me pause. We tend to focus on the negatives; the bad things that happen; or the good things that DIDN'T happen. They overshadow the good that did happen. But, if we pause; if we dare to look back at the peaks instead of the valleys, then it is obvious that God does indeed give us those moments of goodness and joy. God does grant our desires as long as those desires are good for us in the long run. The challenge is to realize that what God has planned for us in the long run is far more rewarding than what we seek to obtain in the immediate near future. God is good and His ways are not our ways. He promises us a hope and a future. He promises to make our lives more abundant and joyful. And, yes, He has gone on to prepare for us a place that seems too good to be true.

You know what, if God seems too good to be true, it is only because He is good and He is true!

CHAPTER 27

*V*ETERAN'S DAY (2013)

Four elderly men stood before me. They had asked to talk to me and I was very, very nervous. One of them was shaking with emotion and all I could think of was somehow I had offended them with something I had written in the play they had just seen.

Let me explain.

In 1993, I was the director of the drama ministry at Brookwood Baptist Church. We produced four dinner theaters a year and my staff liaison requested we sell season tickets for the 1994 season. I was growing tired of writing, directing, and producing plays with a rural flair. I wanted something more modern and urban. I decided on the three plays leading up to our holiday dinner theater for 1994. Then, I wrote down a simple explanation for the fourth play, "The Night Gift". It would take place in an urban setting, a newly constructed high rise in downtown with a penthouse office.

The members of that office would find themselves stuck in the penthouse office on Christmas Eve and in the process discover they didn't get along as well as they thought. That was it. A simple story. I would worry about the details later and write the play sometime during the summer of 1994 in time for the holiday dinner theater.

My good friend and our best actor, Larry Robison, asked me to write him a bit part as an old curmudgeonly gentlemen like Waldorf and Statler of the Muppets. You know, the two old men who sit in the theater box seats and insult the cast of the Muppets show. I created four elderly founders of the company that built the high rise. Larry would play Mr. Collinbird (the others were Mrs. Partridge, Mrs. Turtledove, and Mr. Frenchhen). At a pivotal point in the play, I wanted to change the mood from humorous to serious. Up to that moment, Mr. Collinbird had been hilarious and frankly, senile. The members of the office began to share their most memorable Christmases. When it came to Mr. Collinbird, everyone was expecting another silly story. Instead, he began to tell a very moving story about his childhood.

Mr. Collinbird told the story of Christmas, 1941 when his father did not return from Pearl Harbor. The young boy went out into the woods and cut down the family Christmas tree on his own. During the tale, Larry "became" the young Collinbird and I came out on the stage dressed as his father with blood on my chest. I told my "son" he was now the man of the house and I would not be coming home for Christmas.

It was a simple five-minute scene meant to change the tone of the play and to catch the audience off guard. They would be expecting Collinbird to be silly but instead they got a very poignant moving story of the child who became the man. After the first night's play, Larry came up to me and said there were four men who wanted to talk to the author of the play. These were the four men who now stood before me.

The trembling man wiped at his eyes and this is what he said:

"I wanted to thank you for honoring the men who fought in World

War II. We are World War II veterans and I was at Pearl Harbor. Thank you for honoring us on Veteran's Day."

I was stunned! It suddenly hit me that this was Friday, November 11th, the original date for Veteran's Day! I never intended to honor WWII veterans but God had different plans. God knew who would be there that night and God knew they needed to be honored by the simple scene in this play. The play was performed for two nights only and as impressive and shocking as the first night's response was, I was **not** prepared for what happened the second night.

After the second night's play, Larry escorted an elderly woman up to me and introduced us. She also wanted to meet the author of the play. This is what she said:

"My brother died at Pearl Harbor and I have been mad at him and mad at God ever since. Tonight, you helped me to say goodbye to my brother and to find peace with my Maker. Thank you!"

How do you respond to such a statement? I was truly humbled!

Later, Larry and I spoke about these people and their testimonies. Larry encouraged me to write the story of that young boy in 1941. He asked me where the idea of cutting down the tree as a rite of passage to manhood had come from. I shall share that tomorrow! For now, I want you to stop for a moment and think of someone you know who has fought in our military.

This coming Monday is Veteran's day and 19 years ago, I realized how truly important it is to honor and remember the sacrifice of our men and women in the armed forces. Much has happened in the world since then and the number of war veterans has exploded. It would be a number of years before I fulfilled my dream to take that boy's story and tell it in its entirety.

In 2005, I wrote and produced "The Homecoming Tree" telling the story of the young Mr. Collinbird. The story was based on my parents' lives during WWII. They lived in a boarding house atmosphere and their relatives came to stay with them as the war unfolded. I hope to soon complete the novel based on that play and to fully honor the memories of my now deceased parents. But, for now, I want to encourage you to honor our veterans this coming Monday. Thank them for their sacrifice to give us the opportunity to live in freedom!

Thank you!

CHAPTER 28

THE FALLING TREE

The tree was over twenty feet tall but it had the perfect top. I was freezing and a light drizzle made the ground slippery. Soon, the drizzle would begin to freeze, and my family would find itself isolated in the countryside by a two-week ice storm. Living in the country, our water came from a well and any interruption in electricity deprived us of water. But I wasn't considering this coming ice storm. I was only concerned about our Christmas tree.

It was December, 1966 and I was eleven years old. I was halfway through my sixth-grade year and already, I had grown three inches since the summer. Changes were happening to me that in time I would learn were due to this weird thing called puberty. And, perhaps it was my surging testosterone that allowed me to climb a slippery, icy tree in the cold winds of December.

My father worked for the Post Office. Long before UPS and FEDEX, the post office was the only way to ship packages at Christmas. My father dreaded this time of year. Beginning in early November, he knew he would be swamped at his job.

Extra hours were added to his work schedule. He would leave before 5 AM and not return before 6 PM through most of the month of November and December. Each year, my father and I would go out into the vast wooded area of our 62 acres of pasture and forest and choose a tree for Christmas. The only kind of tree we had to choose from were long needle pine trees. They were never as shapely as a spruce or fir, but they were fragrant and fresh. And, being the poor folk we were, we couldn't afford money for a fancy real tree.

But this year was different. My father had taken on an extra late shift and would be working until midnight for the first two weeks of December. I had the choice of waiting until the end of December to go with my father and cut down the tree, or I could do it myself. I was eleven now. I was growing into a young man, as my mother was fond of telling people. Bolstered by her comments, I was determined to prove myself.

And so, I set out on this dreary gray Friday afternoon looking for the perfect Christmas tree. And there it was before me. Problem was, it was the TOP of a tree! No problem. I loved to climb trees. I would just shimmy up the tree and cut out the top. I had my father's bow saw looped over my shoulder and my fake leather gloves on over my corduroy coat. I started up the tree and was a bit shocked at the slippery limbs. Was that ice forming on the ends of the pine needles? I hoped so. That might mean we would finally have a White Christmas!

I longed for snow at Christmas all my life. I recall one very cold night after watching White Christmas on our new color TV. I was about 9 and I went to the back door of our house. High up in the eaves, my father had mounted a spotlight to illuminate the back yard. I turned it on and leaned out the back door. I craned my neck to look up at that light and waited for snow flakes to drift down around it. It was only days before Christmas. I knew if I longed for it hard enough; if I willed it to happen snow would fall. But the skies were as clear as could be with a million glistening stars against the black velvet of a county side night. No snow. I stood there until I had a crick in my neck and my nose was numb from the cold before giving up and going back into the house.

Now, as I climbed that tree, I said a silent prayer for snow. It would be answered all right. Two weeks of snow and ice and frigid, frozen weather that would close the schools and make our coming Christmas possibly cold and without electricity.

I picked the level that would become the base of the Christmas tree and started sawing away. My hands were already numb from the cold but I soon warmed up as I drew the sharp toothed saw through the soft flesh of the pine tree. The smell of resin engulfed me.

I felt the limb I was sitting on shift and a sudden wind saved my life. I slid to the side just as the tree top above me snapped along the line of my saw cut. The top of the tree toppled to the side and then kicked back with the sharp-edged rim of the saw cut. If I had not slid sideways, the bottom of that toppling tree would have decapitated me. The tree top finally snapped away, the rest of the uncut flesh ripping away. The tree top slid through the limbs beneath me and I fell off the limb.

I clawed at the trunk and the limbs as I slid downward but the now icy bark refused to give my hands purchased. I finally wedged between two of the bottom large limbs and came to a painful halt. The bow saw tumbled down from above me and barely missed my head. I sat there gasping for breath and began to shake. I could have been killed! What was I doing? Risking my life for a Christmas tree?

The feeling of fear and panic began to subside and I felt something new, something fresh. My heart was thumping and my breath was erratic but I had accomplished something on my own. It had turned into something dangerous and I suddenly realized that making decisions on my own would be a risky business. This is what it meant to be grown up; to find yourself faced with a lonely decision and then having to face the consequences. Learn from this, I told myself. Don't ever cut the top of a tree off by yourself. I slowly descended the rest of that pine tree. I found the saw and cut away the ragged bottom of the tree top. By now, night had fallen and the ground was icy as I dragged the tree back across the pasture toward my house.

It seemed like forever by the time I pulled the tree across the pasture to the back of my house. I left it there and stumbled inside to warmth and the smell of fried chicken and mashed potatoes and the warm smile of mother. My father sat at the kitchen table. I was shocked. They had let everyone come home early on this Friday. I told them I had cut down the Christmas tree on my own and the look on my father's face was priceless. His mouth fell open and he couldn't believe it. My mother hugged me and was proud.

Until we saw the tree the next morning in the light of a gray dawn. It was lopsided and crooked and ugly. I was disappointed but my father clapped me on the back.

"We'll make it work, son. It will be beautiful."

There is a photo of me standing next to the ugliest tree we had ever seen for our Christmas. In the following days of darkness and cold without electricity, the fragrance of that tree lifted our feelings. It promised coming days of life and light and the joy of Christmas. The electricity returned in time for Christmas Eve but we didn't go back to school for three more weeks due to a flu outbreak. But, that tree was very special to me. I would lean over and look up through the branches of that tree at the gleaming lights and the shining ornaments and the glistening tinsel and I was once again above the ground suspended above the world; just me and my tree.

Years later, this incident would be the inspiration for that scene in the play, "The Night Gift" I mentioned in my last post. Eventually, I took that scene and wrote an entire play around it, "The Homecoming Tree".

It is the story of a young boy who has lost his father to the attack on Pearl Harbor. He must cut down the family Christmas tree alone so he can become the man of the house. The story revolved around my parent's experiences at the beginning of World War II. I have rewritten the play and I am working on a novelization of the work. One day, I hope to see it on the big screen — it would make a killer Christmas movie! Until then, enjoy your Christmas tree this year. But be careful if you try to cut it down yourself!

CHAPTER 29

THAT DAY OF INFAMY
Written on Dec. 7, 2013

Stop for a moment. Be very still. Shut out the sights and sounds of the world around you. Are you there? Now, recall where you were when the planes hit the World Trade Center. How did you feel? Afraid? Shocked?

Almost thirty years ago, I remember my wife screaming for me to come out of the bathroom to the living room. "They've blown it all up!" she said. I watched in horror as that bifurcated plume of rocket exhaust proved the Challenger space shuttle had exploded shortly after take-off with a school teacher on board.

Some of us can recall an even more shocking moment. I confess that I was but a small child, but talk to anyone over the age of 65 and they can tell you exactly what they were doing and where they were the moment President John F. Kennedy was shot. Fifty years have passed and still the grim and horrifying jerky images of the Zapruder film signaled an end to Camelot; an end to America at its greatest.

But sadly, there are fewer and fewer Americans alive today

who recall when they heard the news that Pearl Harbor had been attacked on December 7, 1941. My parents lived through the Great Depression and moved to a large city from a failing farm in the early 1940's. They are both passed on now, but their stories of the fear and dread they felt when they learned of the attack on Pearl Harbor eclipsed any fear I have experienced since then.

Today, now 72 years later, our memories of that attack have faded and have suffered from the reconstruction of history. Japan is no longer our enemy. Hawaii is no longer a territory and has become the default tourist destination for many Americans. It is difficult for us to fathom the enormity of the defeat of the American fleet on that day. In our day of drones and laser tagged missile attacks and cyber warfare, this kind of attack is unthinkable.

So, pause for a moment and remember the men and women who died that day in a sudden, underserved attack by the Empire of Japan. Stop and recall whatever tiny bit of shock and awe you may have felt in the past few years at other attacks on our country. Be still and say a prayer for our country; say a word of thanks for the men and women who daily put their lives on the line for our freedom.

You see we are free. Freedom and liberty have driven the metamorphosis of our country into what it has become today. Most of those men and women who died that day in Pearl Harbor would not recognize modern America. It would be more foreign to them than any of the enemy countries they fought to defeat. But, there is no dispute in the fact that they would lay down those lives again if it meant protecting the freedom and liberty that has allowed us to grow into the country we are today, good or bad. Let us not take that liberty for granted. For, tomorrow, there could very well be an attack on our country more heinous and more devastating than Pearl Harbor. The question we must ask ourselves:

Do we have what it takes to face such a challenge as did those who fought the Great War against a world filled with evil and death? Let us hope that we do not forget these lessons of history. As Ravi Zacharias once said, "the only thing worse than nostalgia is amnesia."

To the World War II veterans who have gone on to their reward and to the veterans who still live with those bitter memories, we salute you. Thank you for fighting and dying for our liberty. May we NEVER forget!

CHAPTER 30

WHY I WRITE

There is a memory I cherish of a young boy, age 8, walking across a dusty, hot playground. I was that boy and I led a single file line of my classmates towards a small, wood framed house perched on the back corner of our elementary school property in rural Blanchard, Louisiana. It was an old house with worn wooden steps and only one door and one window. As I walked up the stairs, my heart raced and my hand trembled. I opened the old, wooden door and a warm, redolent breeze flowed over me. From inside this house the fragrance of paper and ink and glue; the very blood of books filled my nostrils and I sighed in utter contentment. Here was the universe: here was magic and fantasy; here were worlds and geographies for me to explore; here were men and women and children from the past and all their brave and terrible deeds; here were Books.

In the corner sitting behind a wooden desk was a slight woman with short, dark hair and a ready smile. Mrs. Asbhy stood up and motioned to a nearby shelf of our local branch of the Shreve Memorial Library.

"Bruce, I found a special book for you. You should try it. It is science fiction."

She handed me the book and on the cover were the words "Tunnel in the Sky" by Robert Heinlein. On the cover, an image of a young man, probably 12 stepping through an open doorway onto an alien world beckoned me to follow. I had just held my first science fiction book. I devoured it in one day crouched in the hot cab of my father's old green truck at the end of our driveway along a major highway in Blanchard. In the back of the truck were watermelons. A sign on the windshield advertised them for fifty cents. No one stopped on the lonely highway but I didn't care. I was transported to another world where young people had to survive in a hostile environment after they were accidentally sent on a field trip to a planet no one knew existed and then forgotten. The doorway to my school library opened and I stepped into a new world of adventure as I inhaled book after book. But, as the school year came to a close, I realized the tunnel would soon be blocked and the doorway sealed. Living miles away in the isolated countryside I would not have access to the library. I would have no new books to read.

Growing up on a 62-acre farm of mostly pasture and wooded forest, I had no playmates. I was born late in my parents' life much to the dismay of my brother and two sisters who could not stand the idea that their "mature" mother was "pregnant"! By the time I was a young boy, my sisters had married and moved away and my brother was raising his own family on the same property. For years my nephews were too young to play games and I spent my time wandering through the pastures and piney woods creating stories and playing out scenarios filled with monsters and aliens and creatures of the night. My imagination was fired by books. My sister, Sue taught me to read when I was five. My parents read voraciously. My mother loved romance novels. My father was a huge fan of Zane Grey and his westerns. I read some children's books, but these small, childish stories did not fill my heart with the adventure I longed for. With summer coming, I would have no way to get to the local branch of the library.

One day while re-reading one of my few Superman comic books in my father's truck, I heard a roaring noise. Over the far hill a huge vehicle lumbered through ripples of heat down the hot asphalt highway. It pulled into my driveway and behind the huge steering wheel sat the diminutive Mrs. Ashby. On the side of the vehicle were the words, "Shreve Memorial Library Bookmobile." The library had come to me!

Mrs. Ashby had brought the universe to my house! I will always remember that moment as the door opened and the tunnel yawned deep and long into the world of Imagination. I hopped out of the truck, my comic forgotten and stood on the edge of forever. Mrs. Asbhy smiled and waved her hand toward the interior.

"I have some special books for you, Bruce. Welcome aboard." With tears in my eyes, I walked up the stairs into the hot interior of every tomorrow; of infinite worlds and possibilities. It was then, I knew I wanted to take all the stories I played out each day; all the stories I had heard from my parents and relatives; all the stories I whispered out loud to myself as I fell asleep each night — yes, all of them — and write them down so I could keep them forever in books!

Why did I love stories? I was seven years old when I hid in the hallway behind my aunt's living room to listen to my parents and their relatives tell tales from before the days of the Great Depression. My Aunt Lorraine was a masterful storyteller and she recounted the story of Uncle Dub, an African American sharecropper (although they were not called this in the 1920s) who was hired to watch over the children. My grandfather

Dossie Caskey owned a farm and paid sharecroppers to help with the crops. My mother and her five sisters labored in the hot sun alongside the sharecroppers. Uncle Dub watched out for them.

In the fall, sugar cane was squeezed in a large stone press. The sweet sap would collect in a huge metal vat where it was cooked down to form syrup. One fall when my mother was but a young girl, Uncle Dub was sitting too close to the vat. The fire exploded and hot, boiling syrup covered him from head to toe killing him instantly. Much to the dismay of his relatives, Uncle Dub's skin peeled away leaving him pale, red and bleeding. To hear my Aunt Lorraine tell this horrific story always filled me with dread and fear. I would forever have a healthy respect for a pot of boiling liquid.

As my aunts, uncles, and parents sat around the hot, humid living room underneath buzz fans and lazy flies, they shelled peas and shucked corn all the while spinning stories of a world I could not see. Visions of exploding syrup mills and run away horses and my grandfather's chase across northern Louisiana after those killers, Bonnie and Clyde were far more entertaining than my cousins outside shooting BB guns at rotten watermelons. In that hot, still atmosphere just off the kitchen where fried chicken sizzled in a cast iron skillet, I learned to love the art of storytelling.

And so it was that for Christmas when I was 11, I asked for a portable typewriter. I wanted to write. I wanted to be published. I wanted to be an author! While my friends at school asked for the latest toy or a new baseball glove or football or basketball, I wanted a blank page and a way to put these stories down in permanent format. I wrote my first short story at age 13 for a creative writing class in the eighth grade. It was a shock to learn there was a school topic called "creative writing"! In the ninth grade, I spent six weeks writing everything from haiku to essays. I still have one of my favorite short stories from that year with the most inspiring words I had ever received.

My ninth-grade teacher, Mrs. Griswold wrote in huge, red letters across the top of the first page, "Publish! Publish!" That year I wrote a simple poem inspired by the poem Ozymandias. In my senior year, that poem would win first place in the state of Louisiana.

My senior year I was elected as the Student Council President and was faced with something my parents and siblings never had to consider. Being the number one student in my class, I could have had any scholarship in the state. But, my parents never told me to try out for scholarships. My high school counselor called me into her office in January of my senior year. She scolded me for not applying for scholarships as the best were already gone. I had no idea what she was talking about. I thought you just went to college. It never dawned on me I had to find one and apply to one and then figure out how to pay for it! I told her I wanted to be a writer and she just shook her head. No money in writing, she said. You need to find a real job and write on the side and maybe one day break into the publishing market. She found me a meager scholarship to Northwestern University in central Louisiana, well known for its "humanities". When I left her office, I realized how cloistered and naive this country boy was. I had a lot to learn.

Little did I know that just weeks ahead, there would be a huge change in my life and great and wondrous things would happen. I'll tell you about them soon.

One last thought from C. S. Lewis, author of the Narnia Chronicles. On a midnight stroll through a garden in England, C. S. Lewis confronted his atheism at the request of his dear friend, J. R. R. Tolkien, author of The Lord of the Rings. Tolkien had tried to persuade Lewis to renounce his atheism and embrace Christianity and his final argument stated what Lewis lacked was imagination. After becoming a devout Christian and writing numerous books defending the truthfulness of the Christian faith, Lewis said, "Reason is the natural order of truth; but imagination is the organ of meaning."

Imagine that!

CHAPTER 31

WHY I AM A DOCTOR

Her name is not important but I will call her Sophie. Sophie's skin was thin, translucent like fine white porcelain. Her eyes were teal blue and larger than life. At the age of seven, Sophie had become quite ill with fever and cough that left her listless and lifeless. Even though I was an intern in internal medicine at the time, I was called upon to speak to Sophie's parents. Sophie had a very adult illness. She had leukemia.

Sophie's parents met me in a conference room with cold frosted windows and a bitter winter wind howling outside. This would not be a happy Christmas for this family. I sat down with Sophie's parents and laid out the grim prognosis for their child. We could certainly begin chemotherapy at our university hospital, but eventually Sophie would have to be transferred to a much more specialized hospital. I will never forget the look of utter horror on her parents' faces as they gripped each other's hands and tears rolled down their cheeks. The mother swallowed and said, "We will take Sophie home. If we have enough faith, God will heal her."

I had never faced this dilemma in my budding medical career. What was I to say? After all, I was a Christian and I knew that God could heal. But, really? If Sophie didn't get chemotherapy soon, she would die within weeks. So, I said a silent prayer for words of wisdom and gentleness. And, like a flash, God revealed to me the answer I should give them. I asked a simple question.

"Did you pray for God to heal your child?" Of course, they answered in the affirmative. And then, I told them more of my story.

It was early February of my senior year in high school. I was depressed and confused. Did I really want to go to Northwestern University? So far away from my home town! But, I had to do something. I was determined to go to college and be the first of my family to get a college degree. I walked into the auditorium of Blanchard Baptist Church with some reluctance. Our pastor was a dour, bitter man whose sermons were always so esoteric and lofty, the average rural minded citizen of Blanchard had no idea what he was preaching on. But, our pastor had every reason to be bitter. His wife was essentially homebound with severe arthritis and they had adopted two children from a relative. Those two children were mentally challenged and the man had his hands full just trying to get through the day. It is a testimony to the compassion of his congregation that the church kept him on in spite of his difficulty being an effective pastor. Within a year, I would be the unwitting catalyst of a huge change in this man's demeanor and God would grow him into one of the kindest and most effective pastors the church would ever have. But, that is another story for another day.

ON THIS DAY, he spoke on purpose. Decades before Rick Warren crystalized these thoughts in his bestselling book, "The Purpose Driven Life", Brother Mears laid our a simple but compelling message. He claimed that we were all called to a purpose in life. Yes, ordinary individuals were called by God to fulfill a purpose. Not just pastors and missionaries were called by God which was my prevailing attitude. No, he said, God called some of us to be school teachers, stay at home mothers, ditch diggers, you name it. The important thing is to seek God's purpose for our lives and in finding that purpose, God would give us the desires of our hearts and a life filled with contentment and joy.

IN MY CONFUSED and depressed state, this sermon was just what I needed to hear. Did I have a unique purpose in God's plan? This moment of revelation would be repeated over and over in my life. I would learn the hard way that my tendency was to come up with a plan then hold it up to God and say, "Hey, God, look what I can do for you! So, go ahead and bless it. Aren't you glad I'm on your side! What a wonderful servant you have in me. So, let's get to work with MY plan!" Whereupon, I would end up depressed, confused, and often, flat on my face in failure. I wish I had learned from this early experience in life, but such is the frailty of human memory. We are doomed to repeat our mistakes until wisdom kicks in and we truly learn from our mistakes and we change.

AS OUR PASTOR called for a time of prayer and commitment, I bowed my head and prayed silently. It was a simple prayer.

"God, I'm so sorry I haven't asked this of you before now. I hope it's not too late for me. Just show me what you want me to do with my life." And like the captions in the old Batman television show — WHAM! BAM! POW! — God spoke in my mind, "Bruce, I want you to be a doctor."

WHAT? Wait a minute! I did NOT want to be a doctor. My best friend, Phillip had tried and tried to talk me into being a doctor. I had even accompanied him on some interviews for something called the "six year" program which I didn't really understand because I didn't care! Being a doctor was at the bottom of my list. In fact, it wasn't even on MY list! But, turns out it was the only entry on God's list. And here is the most amazing thing. With that realization that God wanted me to be a doctor came the most incredible acceptance and peace about it. Suddenly, knowing what I was meant to do with my life gave me joy, purpose, contentment. Wow! My life changed in a heartbeat!

The following weeks were a mixed bag of reactions to this event. My parents were totally against it. Two reasons: the money involved which my parents did NOT have and the fact that my life would never be my own. With call and demands on my time as a doctor, I would never get the opportunity to write much less have time for a family. But, I did not let this deter me. When I told my counselor at school, she laughed at me. Northwestern was NOT a prep college for medical school. I shrugged and made a statement out of nowhere, "I'm going to be accepted for the six year program. That way, I'm guaranteed admittance to college AND medical school. Problem solved!" I don't know if she thought I was delusional or inspired. I didn't care. If God wanted me to be a doctor, then I would be accepted in the six year program.

. . .

THE NEXT DAY, I received my letter. I was in. Not only that, but my best friend Phillip was in the program, too. This was unheard of! Only ten people were chosen from thousands of applicants from all over the United States. The idea that two of us from the same high school would be accepted was, well, miraculous! Get the picture! I had NOTHING to do with getting into that program. God deemed it and it was so. This was the first and most powerful lesson I would learn in life. God is in control. No matter how abysmal things may seem; no matter how depressed or confused I might become; no matter how dark the clouds that gather around me; God is always in control.

There is much more to this story of how things worked out to pay my way through college and medical school and an unforeseen scholarship that allowed me to buy a car. And, the list goes on and on.

So, here I sat before Sophie's parents. I told them my story and I reached out and touched her mother's hand. "You see, if you prayed for God to heal your daughter, God reached back through time and touched the heart and mind of this humble physician and called me to be an instrument of healing. You see, I may be the answer to your prayer. God works through people an I am sitting here as an instrument of healing for your daughter. There is no need to take your daughter home and wait for God to work. He is working now, here, through me. Let me give your daughter the treatment she needs."

NICE STORY, Bruce, but what about your dream of being an author? Through those dark, trying years in medical school, writing was my salvation. I kept notebooks of poems and essays; pouring out my pain and fears onto the page; literally bleeding all over the paper. Writing became my way to communicate with God all the conflicting thoughts and feelings as I struggled through medical school and, once again, sought God's purpose for my direction in medicine. None of those writings were published. Not yet, anyway. But, I look back on them now and they are a time capsule of my suffering and doubts and how God took me by the hand and led me through them. They are a reminder once again, that God is in control.

As the years have passed, there have been many, many Sophie's in my life. I can't count all of the times someone has asked me if I am a believer before I put my hands on them and bring God's healing to their lives. I can't count the number of times I have stopped in the middle of a difficult and trying procedure when a patient's life was in my hands and backed away to say a humble prayer for help once again realizing from Whom my strength and calling comes. Why am I a doctor? Because God deemed it.

Sophie went on to that specialized clinic and her leukemia went into remission. I do not know what her eventual fate was. I will never know this side of heaven. But, I do know that in the grand scheme of the universe and the unfolding Story that God is weaving around us, when we put our lives, our future, our ambitions, our plans in His hands, He will lead us and give us a peace that surpasses all human understanding.

Now, the question arises, did I ever get to write again? Well, yes in a most surprising and totally unforeseen way, I did. More on that later. For now, seek God's purpose for your life. It may be simple. It may seem too much of a challenge for you to face.

But, if it is God's plan, then God will prepare the way for you. And, on the other side of that valley of the shadow of death and confusion and uncertainty lies joy, peace, and contentment.

CHAPTER 32

Awake My Soul

A SHORT STORY of hope in the midst of winter's icy grip.

Awake My Soul

I DO NOT MOVE.

I AM QUIESCENT AND STILL.

MOVEMENT FOR ME IS PAIN. Life is pain.

. . .

A Bite of Something Sweet

The trees outside are harsh and bare. Winter has stripped them of vigor and life. Gray fingers claw at the even grayer sky. Even the clouds do not move. The air is still. No wind. No breeze. No life.

My daughter has placed me here on the porch. I feel the sting of cold on my cheeks but I can ignore it. I have ignored all feeling for months now. Since Tom died, I have had no reason to move.

My daughter has wrapped a scarf around my neck and tucked it into the woolen sweater Tom gave me last year for Christmas. I can still smell him on it when I choose to acknowledge my sense of smell.

The air is so cold, it numbs my face. The numbed is numbed even more.

"Why is she out there on the porch?" That is my son-in-law inside the warm house.

"I'm tired of her, Richard. I can't take this anymore."

My daughter has tears in her voice. I cannot feel them. I cannot touch them. The tears mean nothing to me.

"She'll freeze to death." Richard says.

"That's the idea."

. . .

There is a profound silence. And then, subdued sobbing; quiet, subtle. "I didn't mean that."
A white flake shimmies down the still air and lands on my nose. I choose not to feel it melt. So intricate, so beautiful in its design -- one of a kind -- it dies on my cold skin. It dies on the already dead. For, she has left me to die out here alone; cold; still; frozen.

The sliding door opens behind me and a waft of warm air bathes the back of my head. I cannot feel it on my neck for the scarf. Richard's shadow falls over me from the lights inside the house; lights that try in vain to chase away the gray.

"You'll have to forgive your daughter, Mom." He says behind me. "She is very frustrated and wants to leave you out here to die."

"I'm already frozen." I whisper and he leans over me. His breath touches my forehead.

"Did you say something?"

"I'm already frozen." I said more strongly. "Let me finish dying."

. . .

My lips pull apart and I realize they have frozen together. I feel the pain as the first real sensation I have experienced in months.

Richard squats beside my wheelchair and for a second, I choose to notice the strong profile of his face; his angular cheekbones; his gently stubbled chin; his clear eyes. He is watching the trees.

"Winter is hard for all of us, Mom. Spring is coming. I want to tell you a secret. It is a deep and abiding secret that no one can know."

More flakes are falling now and caressing my cheeks. I choose not to feel their gently touch. One lands on my cornea and I blink involuntarily. I must not do that again. But, try as a I might to ignore his statement, the attraction is there. What secret is he talking about?

"What secret?" My voice is a bare whisper.

"Virginia is stressed out because we have chosen to take a journey. It is a long and tedious journey and we will be gone for weeks. She doesn't know what to do with you during that time. She can't leave you alone. And, she isn't going to leave you out here to die." His breath streams away from him, a living thing full of warmth and moisture and the snowflakes eddy and swirl.

. . .

BRUCE HENNIGAN

"Journey?"

"Rawanda. In Africa. There is a little girl. She needs a family." He turns his head to me and his gaze is full and hot on my face. Tears mingle with the snowflakes. "She needs to know her grandfather. She needs to know what he was like. Only you can tell her that."

Another snowflake hits my eye and melts. The moisture runs along my eyelid and I feel a hot tear trickle down my cheek. No! I cannot let this happen! I cannot feel!

"Will you come with us to Rawanda? Will you come with us to get your granddaughter?" His eyes are full and round and wet and the snow is covering his bare head, peppering his shoulders.
 I feel something deep within stir from a slumber of unforgiving anger and frustration. The black dregs of my depression begin to drift away as the warmth stokes itself in my heart. No! I want to scream. No! I want to hold onto the stillness; the inertia; the coming of winter's death. I try to ignore Richard's gleaming eyes and his warm breath and when I subtly avert my gaze a flash of bright red burns my retinas. A lone flower dares to challenge the grayness from my camellia bush. The snowflakes are covering it now and it wants to be seen; it wants to look upward to the hidden sun for life and warmth; it wants to live.

The chair creaks; the ice breaks across my knees and I push, push, push up and out of the heaviness of my crypt of sorrow and I stumble to the flower. I brush away the snow with shaking hands and my tears anoint the petals with life. With life!

Awake my soul!

Awake!

I turn to my son-in-law who is standing with his mouth wide open and the snow covering his head and my daughter stumbles through the open door with her hands pressed to her tear streaked face and I feel the ice crack as I smile. "When do we leave?"

CHAPTER 33

The Innkeeper

I WANT to thank my faithful readers and wish all of you a Merry Christmas and a Happy New Year. To close out 2014, I want to share a very special story with you.

The Innkeeper

THAT NIGHT the trek had been arduous and demanding up the rocky slope to the winding Roman road. I had spent most of the day tending the tenants in my inn but the streets of Bethlehem were so crowded, I couldn't take it anymore. Leaving Lydia behind to tend to the last few customers, I decided it was time to take my annual walk up the mountain.

. . .

A BITE OF SOMETHING SWEET

THE ROAD on the mountain side wound its way past Bethlehem toward the distant city of Jerusalem. They say the Roman roads connected every city in the empire to Rome. All roads led to Rome. And, they say the Romans brought us a more civilized, advanced way of living. But, the cost of that way of life was at the expense of their terrible cruelty. They had given power to our "king", Herod. And, there were times his cruelty surpassed even that of the Romans.

I paused at the top of the winding walking path and stared at the road before me. Rocks were carefully pressed together to make a smooth surface over which the Romans could bring their chariots, wagons, and marching hordes of soldiers. I stepped out onto its surface. The sky was afire with a million stars. One in particular was unusually bright and seemed closer than any star I had ever seen. It cast its light on the empty road. I stood in the middle of this instrument of civilization, this gift to our "backward" people.

I LOOKED out over the small village of Bethlehem. I could see my inn near the edge and for a moment, I thought I heard the distant cry of a baby. Had the woman given birth? The couple had been so desperate, looking for a room. But, the hoards of pilgrims journeying to their home city for the Roman census had swollen the streets of Bethlehem and filled my rooms. I had sent them to the manger. At least there, they would be out of the elements.

I TURNED BACK to the road and crossed to the far side. In the meager star light, I searched the ground. Where was it? Each year, I came. Each year, I sought it. Each year, it became harder to find. Ah! There it was!

. . .

I squatted beside a cluster of rocks and reached out to touch the rough decaying wooden stump shoved deeply into the earth. I ran my hand over the splinters and drew a deep breath as one of them pierced my skin. My blood dripped onto the timber, joining the blood of my brother. This is where they had crucified him. This is where the Romans had made an "example" of dozens of my friends including my hot headed zealot of a brother years ago.

"Why?" I studied the blood dripping from my finger. "Why did you have to die? Why did you have to shed your blood for our people? Don't you see how useless it was?" My hand formed a fist and I stood up as anger surged through my mind. I turned and howled at the empty sky.

"Why, Yahweh, why? Why have you forsaken your people? Why did you let Samuel die on this cruel cross at the hands of these Gentiles? When will you come? When will you send your Messiah to rescue us?" Tears ran down my cheek as my shouts echoed through the canyons and died out in the night.

And then, I heard it. The voices were ethereal, unearthly and musical without being music. I whirled and looked through the empty space where once my brother had hung on a cross along with his rebel friends. From the hilltop came the sound and light began to grow beyond its apex. I stepped over the stump of my brother's cross and made my way up the rocky slope. As I grew nearer to the top of the hill, the voices grew louder washing over me, filling my mind and my heart with awe. What was this?

. . .

THE LIGHT SEEMED FLUID, flowing around me like a gentle stream in a soft rainstorm. I topped the hill with my breath tearing through my lungs, my heart pounding and gazed down in wonder at the shepherds standing on the hill beneath me. Their gaze was turned upward even as mine had been when I had shouted angrily at my God. But, what they saw!

THE SKY WAS FILLED with them; thousands and thousands of beings of pure light and wings and glistening robes and faces filled with wonder and, yes, joy! The song filled the air like perfume. I inhaled it. I bathed in it. I longed for it.

"GLORY TO GOD in the highest, and on earth peace, good will toward men." The words filled my mind. And with them, came a peace, a joy that flooded my wounded heart. The depression and despair that just moments ago had swathed me in a cloud of smothering darkness was blown away like dust by the song of the angels. I fell to my knees. Peace? Could such a thing come? Joy? Would I feel joy again? Good will toward men? Did that mean even the Romans? Even Herod?

ONE OF THE beings of light descended to the shepherds. The angel was with them, but it was suddenly with me, standing before me in all of its glory. I drank in the celestial light and love. I sobbed with the joy of the touch of the divine. The angel's face beamed and it spoke without speaking.

"FEAR NOT: for, behold, I bring you good tidings of great joy, which shall be to all people. For unto you is born this day in the city of David a Saviour, which is Christ the Lord. And this shall be a sign unto you; You shall find the babe wrapped in swaddling clothes, lying in a manger." The angel leaned toward me. "In a manger."

I FELL BACK and covered my face in shame. In a manger? Could it be? Had the Messiah indeed come to us? But, in my manger? Born among animals and filth? My animals? My filth? I rolled onto my stomach and sobbed into the dry earth. What had I done? I had cursed God! I had shaken my fist at Him! I had demanded He do something to relieve me of my suffering. But, it was not supposed to be like this. The Messiah was a king, a conqueror who should have been born in the palace of the high king. Instead, he was born in a manger! In MY manger!

I ROLLED over and the night had once again darkened. I heard a scraping, scratching sound and suddenly the sheep from the hillside were all about me, running, jumping, leaping in joy as they tore over the hill top and descended toward Bethlehem. The shepherds followed. One stopped and reached out a hand.

"WILL YOU JOIN US? Will you come and see this thing which has come to pass that the Lord has made known to us." His face was bright with joy.

I LOOKED AT HIS ROUGH, calloused hand. I grimaced at his odor of night and sweat and sheep. I reached out and took his hand.

"YES. I know where this thing has taken place. In a manger."

. . .

A BITE OF SOMETHING SWEET

THE SHEPHERD SMILED. "Yes. The Lamb of God would only be born in a manger."

HE WALKED PAST ME, leaving me standing alone on the hilltop as he followed the other shepherds and their sheep down into the sleeping town of Bethlehem. He had come that night. He had come in a way I could never anticipate. God worked in ways I could not understand!

I FELT the blood trickle down my hand from the wound in my finger. For a moment, my depression lifted; my despair vanished in the realization that the Messiah had come! My brother would be avenged.

AND THEN, a creeping oppression fell over me. I looked long and hard at the blood on my hand. I felt the splinters of the cross. In a flash, I saw the future, a vision that could only come from God and realized that as painful as it was to have seen my brother die on a cross, it was nothing compared with the pain God would feel when his Son would do the same to save us all. This king was born to die!

I MADE my way down the hill side and stepping over my bother's cross, stepping over the past which I could no longer change; I embraced God's future for us all.

CHAPTER 34

LET IT SNOW

I just posted this on my Conquering Depression blog so I wanted to share it with my reading followers. My wife, at diverse times, is convinced I am crazy.

Okay, so maybe my behavior, at diverse times, is consistent with her conclusion. For instance, it was mid-February. Sherry and I had just returned from a much needed break, a trip to Orlando to relax and have fun and visit our dear friends Mark and Donna Sutton. On a Wednesday afternoon, Mark and I spent several hours brainstorming a devotion book to accompany "Hope Again". In a rather alarming revelation, Mark told me he had gone to have a check up the day before and his doctor wanted to keep him overnight for a cardiac treadmill. But Mark told them he had to keep his appointment with me! Wait a minute, I said. You refused a treadmill because you might have heart problems so you could meet with me?

No problem, he told me. I'll go next week and have the treadmill. Now, where were we?

Back to mid February, the week after we returned. We left a warm, February sunshiny day and returned to a very rare event

A BITE OF SOMETHING SWEET

in Louisiana. On Monday a snow storm combined with an ice storm descended on our fair city. By late afternoon, almost six inches of snow had fallen. And this is where my wife was convinced I was crazy.

You see, I was off a second week in a row and "life" had hit us with as much ferocity as the ice/snow storm. This is why I haven't posted a blog in months! I was stressed out and tired and exhausted and spiritually weakened. Even a trip to Walt Disney World the week before had not lifted my spirits. Now, we were going to be snowed in for a couple of days with no chance of getting out on our icy roads. And, to make it worse, the satellite was covered in six inches of snow so no television! Thank goodness the internet still worked or my daughter would have imploded.

Just before lunch, I peeked out my front door. Huge flakes of snow were tumbling out of a gray sky. I stepped out into the cold and settled into one of my Micky Mouse rocking chairs on our front porch. As I sat down, I realized these rockers were not used often enough. For I was enveloped in quiet. No cars barreled down the road. No construction workers banged and sawed in the distance on the new homes going up around the corner. It was ominously, creepily, deathly quiet!

Why did death have to enter into my mind? Because, Bruce, you are depressed. After weeks of trying to shore up my wife's spirits as we dealt with her aging mother as she was slowly being smothered by dementia, I realized I was depressed. Not due to any particular decisions I had made. Not due to any aberrant behavior. Not due to sliding back into my "stinking thinking" of the past. No, Life was happening and when Life and Circumstances push me into Survival Mode, if I don't pull out of it, I will get depressed. I am aware of this. I KNOW this. I look for the warning signs and when I see Depression sinking its claws into my flesh, I kickstart my Plan and get to work.

Part of my Plan is to turn off the Tech and to retreat from

distractions so I can be still and listen for God's voice. As I sat there in that rocker draped in silence I merely watched as snow fell. It tumbled out of the gray sky in frisky, frolicking flakes. They danced on the still air. At times, the flakes would join into one big clump as if there were more fun in numbers. At times, a lone flake would slow its descent and weave and skate on the air until it managed to make its way under the eaves of my porch to land my knee. It would not last long. I wondered, if it could think what would cross through its frozen mind? Certainly not THAT song! But, would it even know where it had come to rest? Would it be aware of the brevity of its existence? Would it reflect on its journey from heaven to earth only to melt on the warm knee of a troubled human?

The flakes continued to fall and blanket the earth. The dirty brown driveway became a river of glistening white. The dead grass reclined beneath a quilt of newborn white. My wife's camellia bush grabbed clumps of snow with its green leaves and the brilliantly bright red flowers glowed against their white capes. Soon, all was quiet and still to the point I could hear the snowflakes gentle susurration as they bumped against each other.

Be still and know that I am God. Be still, Bruce.

C. S. Lewis talks about a word that describes a transcendent moment in a person's perception when everything around us converges into one incredible awesome revelation of the Divine. Numinous, he calls it. A numinous moment. I have had many in my life. I had one that morning. For as I watched the snow fall and cleanse the air and cleanse the earth, I realized God was cleaning my soul, stripping away the worry, the anxiety, the debris. He was saying, "Bruce, I am here. In the midst of your turmoil, I am peace. In the whirlpool of your sorrow, I am joy. Be still and KNOW me. Be still so I can speak to you through my creation, through my Holy Spirit, through my love. For, Bruce, as I wrap my arms around the world and make it new, I will wash you whiter than snow! Behold, I am making ALL things new!"

I had been on the porch about 30 minutes when Sherry stuck her head out of the door and looked at me in shock. "What are you doing sitting out here in a tee shirt and shorts? Are you crazy?" She asked.

No, I answered, I am at peace!

Two days later, as we ventured out of the neighborhood for the first time, I got a call from Mark Sutton. He had undergone his cardiac catheterization and now, he would have to undergo quintuple bypass surgery the next day! I will share more on that later, but for that moment in time, I was glad I had taken a few moments out of me day to be still and know that He is God! For Life was happening again to my dearest friend.

CHAPTER 35

Thanks, Daddy (2019)

I was born on my father's 41st birthday. I was an "oops" baby. My mother was 37 at the time and had already raised a family. My brother was 18 years older than me. My older sister was 15 years older than me. And, my younger sister was only ten years older than me. But, my parents were convinced they were done building their family. My mother was convinced she was going through the "change in life". In a way, she was.

My father would have been 103 years old on June 13th. He almost made it. He passed away at the age of 98 after a fall from his scooter. He fell asleep waiting for someone he was concerned about. He wanted to escort her out to her car and see that she made it safely. Concerned about her safety and not his own, he fell asleep and tumbled off his scooter. A week later he was dead from swelling of the brain from what is called "the walking dead" syndrome of brain trauma.

When I think of my father, I hardly conjure up images of a loving, hugging, cuddling father figure. His generation did not show their emotions. My father worked for the post office as a mail sorter and spent many long, hard hours in the main post office building in Shreveport, Louisiana. He started that job during World War II and worked right up through the mid 1970's.

HIS GREATEST DESIRE was to be a farmer and he tried his best to do just that with our farm in Blanchard and later, his garden in Saline, Louisiana. Even after moving into assisted living, he raised some of the sweetest tomatoes on his patio in barrels cut in two with his own secret mixture of potting soil and cow manure.

MY MOTHER, particularly during the Christmas holidays, told me many times not to "bother you father when he gets home". He had worked long, hard hours especially during the holidays. My father was never one to play games with me. I don't think he ever threw a ball for me to catch. But, he took me fishing and hunting and he taught me all of his secrets of growing a garden. I have a picture he took of me shortly before I graduated from medical school. He had planted an acre of potatoes. When they were ready, he plowed up the furrows and I would have to walk behind the tractor and toss dirty potatoes into a bag. It was exhausting and very hot work in the central Louisiana summer sun. I sat in the black soil, covered with dirt and potato vines and asked him to take a picture. "When I get done with medical school, you will never see me doing this again!" I proudly proclaimed. Looking back, I probably hurt his feelings. And, I kept that promise.

MY WIFE IS THE GARDENER. Not me. I have no desire to sink my hands into the loamy soil. For her it is therapy. For me, it is drudgery. But, I must confess the thing I miss most about those gardens are the fresh vegetables. And, I have discovered that as I grow older, my parents grow smarter. I would give anything to be sitting in the soil with my father, watching him beam so proudly over an acre of his own hand grown potatoes!

HE TAUGHT ME HARD WORK. He taught me humility. He taught me the need to show my love and approval to my own children. In his latter years after my mother passed away, those inhibitions from his upbringing melted away. He told me time and time again "I love you." And, he would hug me every time we parted. Some old dogs can be taught new tricks. Although, it is not so much new tricks, but a new awareness of the brevity of our existence in this foreign country; our dawning awareness as we mature that other people are so many times more important than ourselves. As Rick Warren said, "It's not about me."

MY FATHER, in addition to being a hard working farmer and post office employee was a bi-vocational music minister. When he stepped behind the pulpit, he transformed! A beaming smile came over his face, his countenance glowed, and his deep, rich voice bellowed out hymns in a fashion that rivaled Tennessee Ernie Ford or George Beverly Shea. I recall so painfully having to move him from his house to assisted living. He fought us because he was afraid he would not have any friends there.

. . .

BUT, once he arrived, he became the song leader for worship services. He found there were many men and women in their waning years lost in their dwindling memories who would perk up and return to the world of reality whenever he would sing for them. He found a latter day mission more meaningful and more powerful than any he had known in life.

WHEN WE HAD to move him into the nursing home end of things, he cried. "I will lose my identity." He said. We made him a name tag so everyone would know him. But, what he soon realized was how he could continue to use his gift of music to minister to those in the other end of the facility. To the day he passed away, he sang hymns and songs to those around him. And, his compassion and concern for others may have led to his ultimate demise. But, what a way to leave this world for the next! I often joked that "When Daddy gets to heaven, Momma's gonna give him hell." Because of all the women he serenaded and ministered to.

You see at his funeral, he had five women honorary pallbearers. And, he sang at his own funeral. He had recorded one of his favorite songs, "There is Coming a Day" to be played at his funeral. It was fitting. It was perfect. It was my Daddy.

AS JUNE 13TH, our birthday, comes and goes and Father Day approaches, I recall my father with the mixed feelings that any son would have for his father. Our fathers were not perfect. And, neither are we! But, I can say that my father left me with a powerful legacy of the appreciation for nature; the appreciating for helping others; and the appreciation of a good song that exists solely to praise our Lord and lift the hearts of the hurting around us.

. . .

BRUCE HENNIGAN

Thanks, Daddy!

CHAPTER 36

*H*OLIDAY STRESS (2018)

I'm facing major surgery on December 4th. That's just three days short of the anniversary of the infamous attack on Pearl Harbor in 1941. Whenever this time of year approaches, I jump into full Christmas mode beginning on November 1. But, this year will be different. Christmas celebration for us will be dialed back a bit.

So, I have already put up our "Homecoming Tree". It is not yet decorated and sits in our living room waiting for its mantle of shiny decorations. This year, Sherry has decided to dig out all of our vintage Precious Moments decorations. Some of these date back 40 years! Decorating the tree will be quite nostalgic!

I guess it is fitting that this is the year I release my novelization of "The Homecoming Tree", a play I wrote and directed at Brookwood Baptist Church in 2005

My Daddy insisted on recording a song for the play. He wanted to sing, "There's a Star Spangled Banner Waving Somewhere", a song original sung by Kate Smith. If you don't know Kate Smith, Google her and see what an amazingly BIG talent she was. My father even helped paint some of the flats for the play. The play premiered in November, 2005 just 15 months after my mother passed away. My father was still mourning her death and at the age of 91, he was trying to "reinvent" himself.

I hope I have that opportunity at 91 to even be able to consider reinventing myself! All of this reminiscing around the play and my father who passed away in 2012 has brought a poignancy to this holiday season. I am now 63 years old, and as Captain Picard said in his first Star Trek movie, "there are fewer days ahead than those we left behind". Or, something like that.

Thus, the legacy of my parents and their generation is memorialized in the book, "The Homecoming Tree". It is now available on Amazon in both print and ebook format. It would make an excellent Christmas present as the story it tells is inspirational and redemptive. I encourage you to pick up a copy and not only read it, but share it with friends and family. For, that is what the book is all about — friends and family.

The last of my mother's sisters, Aunt Billie June, passed away a few weeks ago. There is now no one left of my mother's siblings nor my father's siblings. Their generation weathered the Great Depression and delivered this world from a horrific evil during World War II. Their generation understood sacrifice and the true nature of evil — that is must be fought and banished wherever it is found.

In this holiday season as I face the same surgery my father underwent decades ago, I am warmed and encouraged by the fact I have a great, loving family steeped in the traditions and wisdom of my parents. I have many close friends who will be praying for me and for Sherry.

CHAPTER 37

SCARS AND BLANKETS (2018)

I FOLLOWED the trail of blood from our library across our living room floor. Drops of it had congealed on the carpet in our bedroom leading like bread crumbs to the bathroom. My wife, Sherry, was hunched over her bathroom sink running cold water over her hand. She had cut herself. Again.

LET me pause here and assure you that this was not a deliberate act. Sherry likes sharp scissors. Very sharp. She sharpens them regularly. Why does she like sharp scissors? The better to cut her blankets with. A few years ago, Sherry learned how to make blankets from simple material. Not the intricate quilting most people know about. These blankets were made from two pieces of material with ties around the edge. What made these blankets different from any other involved the process of constructing the blanket. Each tie around the edge is made while saying a prayer for the person for whom the blanket is given.

IN TIME, our library, once the province of my books, was transformed into Sherry's blanket production center. Over the past few years she has produced dozens and dozens of intricately designed, colorful blankets. Each blanket has a singular colored back piece and a very colorful front piece. And the designs on the front she has chosen to match the intended person's personality.

WHEN SHE FOUND there were lots of scrap pieces left over, she developed a way to make smaller blankets as baby burp pads or tiny blankets of dolls. Nothing was wasted.

But, the heart of her endeavors are the prayers and the Bible verses. Sherry developed a laminated card containing the favorite prayers of those who knew the person for whom the blanket was intended. Sherry would ask various friends and relatives for their favorite Bible verses and then place them on a large laminated card attached to the blanket. You see, the blanket was more than just a piece of material. It was a creative act of worship, prayer, Bible reading, and very intentional in every part of its creation.

MY FRIENDS and relatives prayed over the blanket for my surgery.

TODAY, I am sitting on the balcony of our condominium on the beach at Perdido Key, Florida. Sherry and I are talking about the Bible verses we have just read in our morning Bible readings.

A BITE OF SOMETHING SWEET

What you must understand is how creative is our daughter, Casey. She draws. She paints. She creates constantly. It is her way of working through her epilepsy and its emotional toll on her life.

I WRITE. I have written since I was a child. Poems, novels, short stories, essays, blog posts, devotionals, presentations. You name it. In fact, I can't NOT write! It is my way of working through so much going in my tumultuous mind.

FOR CASEY and for me then, creativity is an act of worship; an act of communing with our Creator; a reflection of His creative works in our universe and in our lives.

But, this morning, as in many of our discussions, I reminded Sherry of how creative she is. She doesn't see it that way. She thinks she is just throwing things together. But, this is not true, I remind her. She is using her imagination to visualize the colors and the patterns that best match a person. She imagines which Bible verses best suit that person's needs. And, then, in an act of undeniable creativity, she puts those thoughts; those prayers; that intentional caring into a finished product. This is creativity at its finest!

IMAGINE, if you will, a blank canvas. No, we would have to go to an even more primitive thought. Imagine there is nothing. True nothing. No space; no world; no universe. Imagine God looking down at His hands and thinking and imagining something out of that nothing. It's not something that is thrown together hodge podge. No, this something will need design, structure, laws, order, and most importantly, purpose.

To what purpose? Beings who will reflect God's person; God's image; God's qualities of love and compassion and, yes, creativity. Imagine God blowing into his empty hands a simple breath. This is not just hot air. No, this breath contains all of the potentiality of what became our universe. Stars, planets, galaxies, elements, light, heat, gravity, neutrons — contained in one simple breath; one simple Word as He spoke our universe and all of its complexity into existence.

But, don't miss this one point. Sherry doesn't make blankets for her own enjoyment. Making art for art's sake can become an act of idolatry! No, she is creating for a purpose; for the fulfilling purpose of lifting up a fellow human being. Her act of creativity, while satisfying a need within her own life has the ultimate purpose of satisfying a need in the lives of others. She makes blankets to bring glory not to herself, but to her Savior!

God brought this huge, complex universe with trillions of interacting, moving parts into existence for one reason: for you and me. He designed all of this to give us a home. Everything that has ever happened since the moment of creation until now had been totally intentional.

Everything is "going as planned".
But, the creation is not without cost.

Now, back to the blood.

. . .

A BITE OF SOMETHING SWEET

SHERRY HAD CUT HER FINGER. Again. When Sherry is very active making her blankets and praying over each knot, her fingers are covered with bandaids. If you were to look at her hands, they would be covered with the scars of healed cuts. Each scar is a testimony to her perseverance, her compassion, her unrelenting desire to create something for someone else. She has counted the cost and has not let it stop her.

THERE IS Another whose hands bear scars. These scars ran red with blood from another act of creativity. Oddly, this act of creativity involved something very destructive. It involved death. It involved transformation of something physical into something transcendent. The final product, though scarred, was, in fact the most beautiful sight in the history of the universe. From the tattered remains of a broken, bruised, torn body our God brought forth from the tomb a new life; a new form; a new Way in the person of the resurrected Christ.

JESUS, our Savior, counted the cost of the cross and decided the final product was worth every cut, every drop of blood, every cry of pain. For Jesus Christ saw beyond the creative process to the Finish Line; He saw the power of the empty tomb. God breathed into his empty hands his Word knowing the price of creation would be the death as His own Son on the cross. His love for us; His compassion for us; His desire to embrace us with his unfathomable grace was worth the cost. His imagination far exceeded our feeble grasp of reality.

TODAY, I challenge you to use your imagination; to use your creativity — a reflection of the creative core of our God — and change the world for the better. Write a poem. Write a letter. Send a card — the act of picking it out to match someone's needs is an act of creativity. We are all creative. Count the cost and do not fear paying that cost. The cross was cost enough!

CHAPTER 38

A DADDY'S LOVE

Memory can be fickle at times. What I am sure happened may not have happened exactly the way I now choose to recall it. Many of my memories take on new meaning in the light of future events. I recall one cold, frigid night. My parents were playing Canasta at their friends' home in Buckley Station. Just down the highway from our home, Buckley Station was an anomaly -- a cluster of homes built for those who chose to work at the natural gas pumping station. I am sure the idea was to provide a ready built community for the workers complete with homes on a circular road that enclosed a huge playground for children. Behind the circle of homes was a small lake and a lake house for the use of the occupants of Buckley Station. I suppose there were about a dozen of these houses, all identical in shape and construction differing only with the painting and trim.

I do not recall whose house we were at. I was only four or five. During the evening while my mother and father played cards, an ice storm settled in, bending the rigid trees with glistening hardware and coating the roads with a slick of ice. My father stood at the kitchen door looking at our car. He slowly made his way across the icy driveway and started the car engine to warm up the inside and to melt the ice on the windshield. Minutes later, he held my mother's arm as he led her safely across the ice to the car where he tucked her into the front seat. He returned for me and gathered me in his arms. As he stepped down on the top step of four, his feet slid out from under him.

This is what I recall vividly as if it were yesterday. He clutched me tighter to his chest and tucked his body around mine as he plummeted to the ground. He cushioned my fall and he rolled down the steps onto the driveway. His friends came to help him up and he placed me safely in the back seat of the car. I have no idea if he was hurt. I have no idea if he broke a bone. But, I do know that he risked his life to protect mine. It was in that moment I connected the dots. My father loved me.

Why did I have to connect the dots? My father came from a very stoic family. He grew up during the depression on the farm in Saline, Louisiana. His father and mother showed very little emotion. This was the way of his father's generation. They were born in the aftermath of the Civil War in a country striving to recover its identity and its blood soaked heritage of freedom. There was no time for emotion. The farm was a harsh mistress and demanded all from these men and women. And so, my father never told me "I love you". I cannot recall ever hearing those words uttered by him as I grew up. But, I knew he loved me. His actions showed me that love not only in his protective nature but in his discipline.

I was seven when my sister married and I was allowed to move into my own bedroom, her previous room. My first night in this cavernous room, my father showed up. He placed an old, battered hammer on the night stand beside my bed.

"What is that for, Daddy?" I asked.

"To break the windows out when the house catches on fire." He stately nonchalantly and left my room.

Fire? Windows? I clutched the hammer to my chest suddenly

aware the world around me was filled with danger. And, my father was not going to be right by my side to protect me. I was on my own. I slept with the hammer waking up every hour looking for flames or smoke. A couple of years later, I broke through one of those old fashioned pane windows. It was not with a hammer. It was with my feet. I had jumped off my dresser and onto my bed and turned a somersault. I miscalculated the bouncy nature of my mattress and ended going through the window feet first and out into the front yard. Fortunately, I was not hurt but I was in BIG trouble.

My mother just shook her head and uttered those famous words, "Just wait until your Daddy gets home from work. You better hope he can find an old window to replace that one." He did.

In the years following, I knew my Daddy loved me. He kissed me on the forehead every morning before he walked out the door. But he never said those words, "I love you." I didn't really notice it at the time. Until I was grown.

My Uncle Foots (yes, Foots, because his feet were so big!) was my Daddy's big brother. I noticed the nature of their relationship but it wasn't until I was a teenager that I realized that my Daddy, the baby of the family, desperately wanted his big brother's approval. And, he never got it. Uncle Foots was always, constantly telling my Daddy that anything and everything he did was not quite up to par. There was always something wrong and my Daddy heard the message over and over that he would never live up to his big brother's unreasonably high standards.

It began to bother me but I didn't say anything. Daddy never talked about his relationship with his brother. Or, his two sisters. He just pushed on and did things his way and tried not to sound disappointed. There was something that he excelled at that Uncle Foots could never achieve. My Daddy could sing! I've talked about that in many of my blog posts. When my Daddy stepped into the pulpit (Of the limelight!) on Sunday morning to lead the singing, he transformed! The voice that came out of his mouth was something to behold! Powerful! Loud! Strong! And always, yes always, on key! Uncle Foots could never criticize his singing!

I was twenty years old when Uncle Foots died. He smoked too many unfiltered cigarettes for too long and he developed lung cancer. It wasn't long after his surgery that he passed away. I stood at the entrance to Magnolia Baptist Church arm in arm with my father. My brother, Ronald, stood arm and arm with my mother. I knew this would be hard on my father and mother. What I did not expect what happened next.

Daddy looked at me with tears in his eyes and said, "Son, I love you. You know that, don't you?"

I fought back the tears, not for Uncle Foots loss, but for me! My Daddy loved me! From that day forward, Daddy never ended a conversation without telling me he loved me! We had conversations about his generation's inability to express their emotions. We had a wonderful relationship right up to the day he passed away. That was my Daddy's love! And, I made sure from the moment each of my children were born that I told them every day "I love you."

CHAPTER 39

My First Car

On the Third Day of Christmas
  My True Love Gave to Me,
  Three French Hens . . .

I WAS PROBABLY AROUND four when I got my first car. It was dark green with whitewall tires, fins and double headlights. I didn't just jump right in and drive it, of course. My sister, Sue, took me out for a spin and showed me the ropes. I stayed off the highway those first few days. Unfortunately, that meant I was doomed to try and pedal, yes, pedal my car over the gravel and dirt driveway beside my house. I never reached speeds over 1 mile per hour. In fact, I think I gave up and wished I had a horse, like Trigger, instead.

. . .

THAT'S me below in my cowboy outfit sitting in my car. My sister had a horse named Babe so why couldn't I have a horse? After all, Roy Rogers and the Lone Ranger had horses. They didn't drive little green cars around their yard. But, at the age of four such depths and intricacies of life were beyond me. I was more worried about my next meal and my next bowel movement than I was my little green car. I came late to potty training. Sorry. TMI.

TWO YEARS LATER, my Daddy moved me up the ladder from the car to a tricycle. Red and white with little streamers on the handles. I still wore a cowboy outfit. But, now, I was the Sheriff. I wore my star with pride. I could barrel around the backyard at 2 miles per hour. The larger wheels made negotiating the bumps and clumps of grass in the yard easier and I seldom got stuck down in a red clay rut in our driveway. But, as all true cowboys do, I grew restless with my ride. I wanted something larger.

I WAS ABOUT seven when I got my first bicycle. I those days, there were no such things as hand brakes. A hand brake was what happened when you fell off the bicycle and tried to stop yourself from sliding across the pavement. You had to push backwards on the pedal to stop the bicycle. This required that your legs would be long enough to reach from the seat to the pedal. Now, my mother, ever one to plan and procrastinate decided she would buy me one bicycle for my entire life. She purchased a huge, adult size bicycle that Christmas. It was red and silver and the seat was even with my nipples. I had to climb on the back of our old green car to get into the seat and then push off.

. . .

A BITE OF SOMETHING SWEET

RIDING IT WAS A CHALLENGE. My brother-in-law, Wayne, ever patient and vigilant taught me how to ride. We had one telephone pole in the front yard. Just one. I was supposed to stay on the driveway but for some reason, like a magnet, I was drawn to that pole. As I stood up on the pedals (because I couldn't reach the seat) I wobbled to and fro and found myself pulled as if a mighty rope were uncoiled across the front yard and I ran right into the telephone pole. I sat there stunned for a second because the blow had knocked me up onto my seat and then I fell over into the open sewage line that ran across my front yard.

I RODE that bicycle until I was a senior in high school. It served me well and though it was a challenge at first, I grew to love it. I learned to ride up the hill where my mother parked her school bus and rush down the rocky, bumpy dirt hill to rocket across the driveway past the back porch, down the walking lane to my sister's house and around her tiny driveway to the back driveway that ran by the trash can where the day's trash was burning, through the lane behind my brother's taxidermy shop where the blue flies buzzed and flew down another short hill and then to the right up to my brother's house where the momentum would carry once again to the top of the hill by the bus.

MY MOTHER WOULD NEVER LET me ride on the highway, but I wore the ruts into those red clay driveways and walkways. I look at these pictures now and they seem so far away. Those memories are distant and if I stop and concentrate, I can pull them back into some brief focus and smell the pine sap in the air and feel the heat on my face and taste the dust in my mouth.

. . .

EACH YEAR, we make lists and we count our cash or watch our credit card limit swell as we prepare to give presents for Christmas. Some of these presents are truly memorable. Others are quickly forgettable and are either "retired", "regifted", or given away to a stranger the next year. One year at a "white elephant" party someone passed along a Santa with gas. When you poked his belly he emitted a nasty sound. That Santa made the rounds at annual Christmas parties for years. Somewhere along the way it mercifully got lost in the trash.

THREE FRENCH HENS make no sense to us today. But, in the days this song was written, French hens were a very expensive delicacy and would have been a gift fit for a king and so they represent the gifts of the magi. I am sure that Mary and Joseph were shocked when majestic, kingly strangers appeared at the door to their house inquiring about their son. Jesus was a toddler at the time. He had long ago moved out of his swaddling clothes. I am sure that Mary and Joseph, still in Bethlehem, had already begun to wonder where this surreal journey of life with the Son of God would take them. Perhaps the memories of the angels and the shepherds were already growing dim. Maybe it all seemed like a distant dream. And then, God reminded them again of their special duty.

THE KINGS SHOWED up with three unusual and unwieldy presents. Like my car, tricycle, and bicycle were so unfit for dirt roads and life in the country, their three gifts must have mystified Mary and Joseph. Gold, they understood. Gold could be put to good use. But, why give them gold? Gold was a gift for a king. And, myrrh? Myrrh was an oil for anointing the dead. It was expensive but hardly useful for diaper rash. Frankincense was an incense. It could be burned and make the house very fragrant, which given the nature of some of the young Jesus' typical childhood "messes" might come in handy. But, frankincense was meant to be burned as a pleasant fragrance to God, the father. What were they to do with these three gifts? Certainly, they could not give them to Jesus at playtime.

AND SO, like her cherished memories of the visit of Gabriel and the shepherds, Mary put the gifts away for the future. God would show her how to one day use them for their family. Perhaps they would have to leave this small house in Bethlehem and the gold would give them enough money to move to another place. Perhaps the frankincense could be offered as a sacrifice in the temple, something Jesus may one day understand. And, the myrrh. Should she save it for Jesus' funeral?

I CAN SEE Mary standing in the doorway of her small home as the magi disappear into the distance. Jesus is barely walking now and is toddling along the dirt street waving to the disappearing men who gave him such strange gifts. I can see a shadow pass across her face as the morning sun casts a symbol of dark forbidding on the ground. Eclipsed by his upraised hands, waving goodbye to the kings, her son's shadow has placed a cross on the ground before her. She shudders with a terrible premonition that perhaps she will outlive her son. Clenching the myrrh to her bosom, she will put it away with all of her thoughts and fears and place her life in the hands of the Father. And, when Jesus turns and smiles at her and calls her "Momma" she smiles back and hides the tears.

CHAPTER 40

𝓑OLDLY GOING FOR 50 YEARS (2016)
   My father was obsessed with television sets. During the football season, he would have three televisions going at the same time and be listening to a game on his transistor radio. This was long before cable when we could get only three channels way out in the sticks of Blanchard, Louisiana. In 1965, he did something unthinkable. You've got to understand our financial situation back then. My mother had a job — not a common thing to have both parents working in 1965. She drove a school bus and my father worked at the post office. We weren't rich at all. We lived in the country and raised most of our food in my father's garden. To give you an idea of how poor we were, one year I wanted the newest toy sensation, Creepy Crawlers. You purchased the box and it it was a small "oven" that heated up metal molds with shapes of various insects. The set came with gooey plastic in a bottle you could squirt into the molds in various color combinations. Then, you put the molds in the oven and pressed the timer. In minutes, the opaque colorful liquid would harden into a translucent rubbery substance. You

peeled your creepy crawlers out of the mold and you had instant vermin!

I wanted this for Christmas so bad. My mother and father pooled some money and bought me an expansion pack instead. Four molds and three bottles of goo. But, no oven! The expansion pack was much cheaper than the whole box. So, here I was on Christmas morning holding my little metal molds over the fire in the fireplace to make my creepy crawlers. Over and over, the things would catch on fire! It's a wonder I didn't suffer third degree burns!

Back to 1965. My father came home from Sears and Roebuck store with a huge cardboard box in the back of his old green truck. Much to my mother's dismay, he had spent a pot load of money on something new. Something big! He and my brother loaded the box into the living room and my father revealed a huge console television. But, it wasn't just any huge television (Only 24 inches screen — a baby compared to today's monsters) it was a COLOR television!

Over the next few months I was stunned and amazed at the color images that flickered across the screen. Not all shows were in color. Certainly, Walt Disney's Wonderful World of Color was! My favorite show at the time was still in black and white — Lost in Space. I was a science fiction fanatic and couldn't wait each week to hear those famous words uttered by the robot, "Danger, Will Robinson!"

In the late summer of 1966, one of my mother's new TV Guides arrived in the mail. For her, it was a little bit of Hollywood glamour in the red clay and pine hills of northern Louisiana. She loved to do the crossword puzzle which featured the names of famous movie and television stars. This TV Guide carried the image of two men dressed in gold and blue tunics with the title of a new show underneath. "Star Trek". Star Trek? What was this? A new science fiction show in color! I read about the show set on the starship Enterprise with its leader,

Captain Kirk and his alien first Officer Mr. Spock. Mr. Spock? Wasn't that a famous children's doctor?

On a cool September night, September 8, 1966 at the age of 11 I had finished my supper and was settling down on our couch in front of new color television. My mother and father were off doing something around the house. I guess I'm fortunate there were no Westerns on that night or I would have never seen this new show. The screen came to life with vibrant color — reds and golds and blues and exotic planet sets that blew my mind. I watched as this doctor, "Bones" McCoy showed up in coruscating sparks of light along with his Captain Kirk on a lonely planet to meet his long lost girlfriend who had married an extraterrestrial archeologist. The opening of the show was so ordinary and yet so exotic as if it was perfectly normal for someone to "beam" down from a starship onto the surface of an alien planet. There were no silly sayings or rambling robots. This was pure drama, straight to the heart of real characters. In later years, this paradigm shift would be responsible for me leaving behind the childish comic books of DC for the more mature comes of Marvel. I was enthralled, gripped, captured by the story that unfolded before me. The red shirt ensign getting the life sucked out of him by the beautiful woman who was Dr. McCoy's love. How could SHE be a monster? She looked so normal and so beautiful! And, then the big reveal. At the end of the show when McCoy's girlfriend is killing his Captain and we see the thing for what it really was! Oh my! I ran and hid behind the couch. I was traumatized but captivated. I could not believe my eyes. This was the most amazing show in the history of shows!

"Space, the final frontier. These are the voyages of the starship Enterprise. It's five mission: to explore strange new worlds, to seek out new life and new civilizations; to boldly go where no man has gone before!" Then that fantastic fanfare with the

A BITE OF SOMETHING SWEET

warbling vocals almost alien in tone. To this day, it gives me a thrill.

I never missed an episode of Star Trek. I wrote a letter to stop its cancellation. Dr. McCoy would become my role model when I decided to become a doctor. I can say that my life was deeply affected by Star Trek. The three main characters for me represented the three aspects of our personality. Mr. Spock was the cold, calculating intellect, the superego. Captain Kirk was the visceral, go from the gut leaders the id; and Bones was the humanity, the heart that brought the two extremes together. My love for science grew out of Star Trek. My desire to be "just a plain old country doctor" came out of my love for the character of Dr. McCoy.

In 2008, I had the pleasure of meeting Leonard Nimoy at Book Expo America. I snapped a picture of him but did not have the privilege of getting a picture with him, but I did shake his hand and thank him for the character of Spock that so shaped and influenced my life. I missed out on seeing William Shatner during that trip and unfortunately, DeForest Kelley who played Dr. McCoy had passed away a few years before.

Fifty years have come and gone. I've sat through every movie, every animated episode, every spin off. In 1996, I took my son, Sean, to Pasadena California for the 30 year celebration of Star Trek and met many of the stars of Next Generation and Voyager. He dressed in a Star Trek costume that year.

So, to honor Star Trek and its fifty year anniversary, I spent a lot of money and went to Dallas FanExpo in June to meet William Shatner. What a pleasure and a joy to actually meet Captain James Tiberius Kirk. Here is the photo I had made with Willam Shatner and notice the tee shirt I'm wearing.

Here's to another 50 years of "boldly going where no man has gone before!"

CHAPTER 41

A VISIT WITH TEETER AND GOOFER!

I HAD THIS IDEA. At the time, I was convinced it was a good idea. Sherry and I had spent our honeymoon in Walt Disney World and had been going there off and on for twelve years as of 1992. That year, my father was 78 and my mother was 74. But, I really wanted them to experience the fun my family was having at Disney World. By 1992, Sue's family had been with us and she had become a Disney fanatic. Shortly after, Gwen (and later her whole family would go) had been and had also become a Disney fanatic. So, I reasoned, why not take all of them with Mother and Daddy to Disney World. Well, on this trip, Sue and Gwen would go with me, Sherry, Casey (5 at the time), and Sean (8 at the time) as we would take Mother and Daddy to Disney World. We chose a down time of the year. If we arrived the Saturday before Thanksgiving and left to come home on Wednesday we would be the Thanksgiving crowds and have four days at the parks. At that time, there were only three parks, Magic Kingdom, EPCOT, and Disney Hollywood Studios. All we had to do was get there. Yeah, right!

BELIEVE IT OR NOT, the only way I could get us all down there was to rent an enclosed trailer and put all of our luggage in it so that we would all fit in the van. Then, get Sherry and the kiddos to fly down and we meet them at the airport. We also stayed in the old Disney Village Bungalows which have since that time been torn down and replaced by Saratoga Springs Vacation Club Villas. We ended up moving to these new villas called Vacation Club since renamed Old Key West because of the screaming family we could hear through the walls at all hours. Mother and Daddy ended up sleeping in the two bed room with Gwen and Sue in the other bed. The kiddos slept on the couch and Sherry and I ended up with a king size bed and our own room. So far, so good.

IT WAS A WONDERFUL TRIP. No doubt about that. Mother and Daddy rented scooters so they wouldn't have to walk to far. But, often to get Mother to the scooter, we had to use a wheelchair we brought from home. I will never forget pushing Mother in the wheelchair up the LONG ramp at the Wilderness Lodge. That ramp must have been at least a half a mile long!

MOTHER AND DADDY just loved seeing the Christmas decorations all over the park. If you've never been to Disney World at Christmas, you are missing the most beautiful, clever Christmas decorations in the world!

. . .

BRUCE HENNIGAN

SOME MEMORIES:

WE ATE at Alfredo's Restaurant in Italy (EPCOT) because I knew Mother and Daddy ate lasagna. The meal went find until mother asked the waiter "Do you use Prego on the spaghetti? It's real good." And, Daddy took out a Snickers bar to eat for dessert instead of one of the signature desserts.

ON SPACESHIP EARTH, the final descent from the top of the sphere takes place with the car spinning around backwards so that you are leaning back as the car moved downhill. Daddy couldn't take going backwards so he stood up in the car and turned around and crouched on the seat facing backwards (or, in the real sense, forward).

WE ATE at the Prime Time 50's Café in Disney MGM Studios. This wonderful establishment features décor from the 1950's complete with black and white television sets in every "dining room". Playing around the clock are excerpts from 1950's television shows. The décor reminded me of Mother's decorations at home and most of the shows I had watched as a wee child growing up.

BUT, the most fun at the café comes from the servers. They pass themselves off as you "sister or brother" and talk about "Mom is cooking lunch in the kitchen." Then comes the rules. No elbows on the table or you stand in the corner. And, the servers make you stand in the corner! Eat all your vegetables or you get the "airplane" delivery of at least one bite! And, if you can't tell the server the color of the soap in the bathroom, that means you didn't wash your hands and it is the corner for you!

OUR FAVORITE SERVER of all time was Ghassan. Ghassan recognized us every time we walked in the door. His shout of "Hello, Seester and Brother!" brought joy to my heart. And now, he was to meet Mother and Daddy for the first time. I have the meeting on video and it is so heart warming, so wonderful, so much fun to see Mother, Daddy, Sue, and Gwen interact with our "brother" Ghassan. Ghassan would be moved to other restaurants over time and we always followed him no matter where he served. EVERY time, he recognized us (Mostly Sue) and hugged us. The last time we saw Ghassan, he was working at Boatwright's restaurant at the then name "Dixie Landing" property. He announced he was getting married and moving to New York City. Sue, Gwen, and myself were the last ones to see Ghassan. I really miss him and wish him blessings wherever he and his family are.

WE MISS YOU BROTHER!!!!

BUT, the best took place at EPCOT. We were going around the World Showcase and we had just eaten in Italy. Mother and Daddy drove their scooters into a crowd of characters. Tigger, the bouncy Tiger from Winnie the Pooh jumped onto the scooters, putting one foot on the foot rest of each so that he was stradling both scooters and took over, driving my Mother and Daddy away into a huge crowd at EPCOT. The last thing I saw and heard was my mother, waving her arms in desperation screaming, "Bruce, help us." And, they were gone!

. . .

I RAN through the milling crowd, bouncing from person to person sort of like my own pudgy version of Tigger until I arrived at the Japan pavilion. There, a huge crowd of charactes were gathered around something. It was Mother and Daddy! The characters were laughing and dancing all around Mother and Daddy's scooter. When I arrived, they parted and my Mother grinning from ear to ear said, "Bruce, meet my new friends Teeter and Goofer." Of course, she was referring to Tigger and Goofy but I did not correct her. They were having the time of their lives! I still remember and cherish that singular, giddy moment of magical joy. And every time I see Tigger or Goofy, I recall their new names bestowed upon them by my Mother!

ON THE WAY BACK, we spent the night in Chipley, Florida at the only motel off the interstate. The next day, I could not find my backpack with my wallet and the keys to the van! Where was it? I went outside and I had placed it on the fender of the trailer in plain sight of anyone walking by. God was watching out for us for anyone could have walked off with the keys to the van and my wallet! That day was Thanksgiving and we stopped on the way home and ate a Thanksgiving meal at a restaurant. We were together for Thanksgiving and we had a memorable time.

I IMAGINE THAT IN HEAVEN, Mother and Daddy have run into Walt Disney and have probably thanked him for Disney World. Only Mother would have advised him he should have used Prego on the spaghetti!

P.S. WE WENT BACK in 1994 for Sue's 50th birthday and to

celebrate Daddy's 80th birthday. We didn't bring a trailer that time!

CHAPTER 42

*C*hristmas Eve Menu
 Gwen's Chicken Salad Sandwiches — her secret? Use candied sweet DILL pickles.

SUE'S MEATBALLS — Small meatballs in Heinz Chile Sauce and grape jelly in a crock pot.

SUE'S LITTLE SMOKIES — Little smoky sausages in barbecue sauce in a crock pot.

DATE LOAF — Sounds strange but this candy made with milk, sugar, pecans, Karo syrup and dates forms a "log" wrapped in a moist kitchen towel and then cut into half moon slices is so good!

. . .

A BITE OF SOMETHING SWEET

Shine's Fudge — Sherry's mother's recipe for fudge from an old cake icing recipe.

Mamaw's Divinity — not sure where this recipe came from but my mother and I made this divinity EVERY Christmas and it is very difficult to get just right but when you do! Oh my! Little clouds of heavenly sweet stuff!

Lena's Pralines — Mother found this recipe on the back of a bag of sugar and I still have that recipe. Uses buttermilk but makes the BEST pralines ever! Hard to make because it foams up so much!

Home made Millionaires — made from melted caramel, toasted pecans and melted chocolate coating. Now we make little Rollos on pretzels and pecans. Much easier but not as good.

Punch — Mother loved this punch. Simple. Lime or Pineapple sherbet and ginger ale.

Texas Trash — The original Chex cereal mix with lots of pecans!

Minnie's Prune Cake — Wait a minute! Don't write this off. From my mother's mother, this is the most moist and lusciously spiced cake you'll ever eat. And, after Christmas meal this will insure that things move along the way they should!

. . .

TOFFEE BARS — This recipe so simple comes from graham crackers, chopped pecans, and syrupy mixture cooked in the oven. Let it cool and break it up and it is so good.

CHAPTER 43

Much to my amazement one of Sean's friends passed on to me a transcript from an interview he did with my father. I had no idea this existed until after my father passed away. I have left it unedited just as my father said it. It is HIS story of HIS life in HIS own words!

THE LIFE AND TIMES
   OF
   D.S. HENNIGAN
   IN HIS OWN WORDS
   TRANSCRIBED FROM AN INTERVIEW BY
   ROBERT PARKER

I'VE BEEN ASKED to say a few words into this tape recorder. I can't write very well and I can't talk any better than I can write. So, anything that I say here, as far as to the right construction of paragraph, or sentences or anything of that nature is purely coincidental. I probably won't get the right words in the right place to describe my thoughts and what I feel.

LIFE -- GOD'S MOST PRECIOUS GIFT

THE FIRST THOUGHT to come to me is the word, LIFE. Life is the most precious thing, obviously, that we have on this earth. There's an old saying; "the sweet mysteries of life." I think about that's not all together true; another word enters into that, which makes it the "sweet and bitter mysteries of life." I guess a mystery is something that is not immediately solved when we're confronted with it, and while in our later years, or days, it might be revealed to us what the true mystery is. I think sometimes in life some of the mysteries are not ever solved. We have to leave that up to God, I think. Somewhere down the line, when we pass from this earth these mysteries we have do not ever get solved and don't understand, that we'll understand them then.

PAUL SAID, "Now we see through a glass dimly, but then we shall see him face to face." Which makes us believe that we'll understand all things by and by. Without life, there would be no majestic snow-capped mountains for us to view.

MOUNTAINS

MOUNTAINS COME to my mind because it seems to me that mountains are of the most in my love for God's handiwork. I like to view them at a distance. Or on a safe road. I never particularly cared about being in a drop-off to view a mountain, but in a safe place it is really uplifting and inspiring to me. I think that it should be that way because God, when he gave Moses the ten commandments, gave them from a mountain, and when Noah landed the ark it was on Mount Ararat. I believe and I think his transfiguration happened on a mountain. One of the prophets said "I will look unto the hills, from which commeth my help," which I think refers to God. I think the mountain, in all of it's beauty, in all of it's splendor, is the handiwork of God. When He made them, it may not have been all in one day, but he could have made them in one day, had he wanted to. I think only the finger and the hand of God could have carved out the canyons and rocks and painted them different colors that makes them so endearing to us, as we view them. So, I have in my heart a special place for God's all-inspiring mountain, and I think it was a superior being that created them.

GRAND CANYON

WITHOUT LIFE, we would not be able to view the wonders of one particular spot, the Grand Canyon, which is one of the seven wonders of the world, in all it's beauty and different colors. It is a deep hole in the Colorado River that winds through the Grand Canyon, and God's hand, I think, could have carved that out. Of course, in time, God's elements -- wind, snows, and what ever has riveted it into the canyon it is today, but I think God is due all the credit; and also between each mountain he saw fit to draw a line and make a valley with beautiful streams flowing fast down these valleys, which is also inspiring. We think about "the shadow of the valley of death" when we think about in Psalms, even though God would go with us though all these things, but we enjoy the valley that God has carved out. Some of them are carpeted with green grass and scattered trees and it seems that God uses wild flowers to tack down that carpet to keep it in place with those beautiful wild flowers. I'm only speaking from experience of places that I've seen, especially a new toiled field or beautiful green valleys with fine, flowing streams, which are refreshing, that runs through those valleys. I think that's one of God's great handiworks.

THE DESERTS

AND THEN, not to forget the deserts, because I've been across those deserts with their blue haze. As you see for miles and miles across that desert that is flat, and then you see a mountain behind it. The desert has it's inspiration, I think, because there are dry areas in our life that we go through and that we've experienced hardships, but in the end we reach the mountain where the cool air and the water and the breeze is. Most times we find trees and flowers of different types on those mountains, so that the desert within itself is beautiful. The Painted Desert is a beautiful place that God chose to carve out that we might enjoy -- the Petrified Forest --so many things that we would not enjoy if it were not for God.

DO NOT FORGET the beautiful sunsets, the beautiful sunrise, as the clouds in the sky reflect back the colors of the sun; the different oranges, yellows, and reds that thrill our hearts to observe. We also have the pine belt in Louisiana, in Arkansas, in East Texas, and Mississippi. We enjoy those pine hills. They are beautiful. Even the Ozark Mountains and the Smokey Mountains, God saw fit to make, which are different from the Rocky Mountains. Sometimes the Rocky Mountains are barren and have no vegetation because of the altitude. The Smokey Mountains and the Ozark Mountains do have the vegetation that makes them beautiful.

WE ALSO SEE THE OCEAN, with it's waves coming into the shore. Sometimes it's rough with the waves that roar in and then again it's serene and smooth, which reminds us of the way life is sometimes. The waves get pretty high, and then when we trust in God, these waves become smooth in our lives because some of the problems have been smoothed out and seem far-distant.

THERE ARE SO many things if we didn't have in life we would not enjoy: the stars, the moon, and the sunshine, flowers, even the children as they paddle around the house with their smile and their laughter. Of course, they are called brats sometime, but that's just what we call them and we don't mean to be mean about it. We try to head 'em in the right direction, correct them and discipline the way we think they ought to go. We enjoy those things. Without them life would be void, I think, of course, some people choose not to have them. But, I don't think that's a good idea.

AGAIN, we have the summer, the winter, the spring and the fall. The spring and the fall, I suppose, are the most beautiful; with it's flowers in the spring and the green trees, and then in the fall, the colored leaves, and then eventually, we have a snow flake or two, which we enjoy, but no too much of it. So many things in life reveals unto us that we enjoy. That is the reason that life is so precious to us.

. . .

EVEN THE STORM CLOUDS, as they roll up into the sky, the lightning, the wind, it shows some of the power that God has, even thought sometimes it is destructive. We are inspired by it, we have a tingling of the spine when we see these come up, knowing that God has all power. He can cause the oceans to be rough, but he can also still the storm and calm the waters in our life. Life is most precious.

MY LIFE -- BEGINNINGS

THAT LIFE CAME TO ME, June 13, 1914, through William Daniel Hennigan and Linda Mae Britt Hennigan from Saline Louisiana. I did not ask to be born into this would. I had nothing to do with it, as all of us do not have anything to do with being born into this world. We have nothing to do with it and can do nothing about it. We were not asked who we wanted to be born to; our parents, whether they are rich or poor, whether they were ugly or beautiful, or mean or good, so we don't know. We were born to them anyway and in most times and most cases, even if they were poor, they were our parents. We knew nothing else except this so we loved them. And they loved us. I am reminded of a quote, which I hope to read part of, which I think fits very well that of a newborn babe. It is a quote from a professor at LSU.

"WE ARE EXPECTING a baby soon in our family, our eighth grandchild. Excitement is rising and feelings are stirring. Hope is swelling around the anticipation. It is remarkable how the birth of a baby makes everyone feel more alive, more tender. It then makes us gentler and kinder. Some have speculated that at birth a baby's skin is so tender that it can feel the pulsation of the stars and planets, as well as the vibrations of radio, TV and microwave signals. There is an old Jewish saying, 'in the womb, the child knows eternity, after birth he forgets it.' The newborn child slowly grows tougher. The skin gradually tightens and hardens. This is all a necessary process, because the human infant is the most dependent, for the longest time, of any creature. He is also the most defenseless, helpless, and needy. God has built the necessary defenses against too much bombardment of the child's receptors, such as skin, ears, eyes, etc. Leaving from the uterus to the outside world is a powerful physical shock for a baby. In the womb, the fetus is protected from light. The sounds are cushioned and food is present before they feel any hunger.

"THEN COMES THE BIRTH EXPERIENCE, often painful for the mother and must also be painful for the child. The birth canal is so narrow that the child's head is squeezed to a point that the face and forehead are often scratched so that the baby has swollen eyes and bruised faces shortly after birth. They nearly all come from the womb with a cry of protest. Think of the difference between the warm, comfortable, secluded shelter of the mother's body compared to the outside. While once all was quite, dark and peaceful, now there are bright sights and noises, hoarse voices, shouts, sneezes, jerks, cold sheets, wet diapers, sharp pins, wrinkled hands and hunger pangs. A lot of change in such a short time span. The birth of a baby comes as close to any place or time when heaven touches earth and is a pure miracle. Small wonder that one of our greatest Christian celebrations is around the birth of Jesus. We need to celebrate it over and over because it is always God's spirit that mellows our compassion. Attempts to rehumanize us again and again."

. . .

BRUCE HENNIGAN

NEWBORN BABIES

SPEAKING OF A NEWBORN BABY, we know that it is wholly dependent on it's parents, and it's brothers and sisters to take care of it. For several years, it has no way of communicating except by when it hurts or when it's hungry it cries. And when it's happy, it laughs and kicks and makes funny noises, so, it does have a way of communicating with us.

I SPEAK this way because I want everybody to realize how important and precious a life can be and I think we have talked about that throughout this little skit I spoke about here. It is very important that we, as parents, steer our children in the right direction, in order that they might become better citizens and better Christians. Of course, you can't do much with them until they get to the age of accountability and know right from wrong and then you try to teach them right from wrong and help them grow in the right direction.

I THINK a good way to start a child off is in the church. I don't think you ever go wrong with that. But the real importance should be stressed not only to the child, but to the parents about what this child means to the world, because once you're born into this world, the world is never the same. You change it, one way or another. You change the lives of those around you. Your loved ones, your mother and your daddy, because they have someone else to love and care for, someone else to worry about in sickness and in health and happiness and also your siblings, your sisters and brothers and friends and loved ones that you come in contact with, their lives are changed. So it is very important that we stress this to the child and to the parent how

A BITE OF SOMETHING SWEET

important this is, because we have the example. Many people who are just babes at one time depending on somebody else for their life support and we can name a few of them that had an adverse affect on the world --Adolph Hitler, Mussolini, Sadam, and even in the First World War Germany was the only thing I can remember. They really changed the course of the world and people's thinking.

AND ALSO, though I don't know them, we had very important people like Billy Graham, George Washington, Eisenhower, and many that I could name that changed the course of the world and humanity. Thomas Edison and Benjamin Franklin.

WE SHOULD BE VERY careful and stress to these people how important their lives are. Even though we think we don't have much influence on the world we do have. I never did realize that to not have that family, probably when we all got together, there would be thirty-something' of us, which was brought about by me being born in this world. All of these people's lives I touched and all of them were related to me in one way or another. So, we never know what our lives are going to amount to. Even my children, as they work from day to day, come in contact with many people and I think they are all good and they have a good influence on the people that they know. Of course, Bruce being a doctor, he has a very important job of doctoring people and trying to cure them of their ills. Of course, Gwen, with her company, comes in contact with people around the city who deal with businesses and they know that she has good character and is a good woman. Sue, working in the school, has direct contact with the kids and she has an influence on them for good, and I hope never for bad. Ronald contacts people through his sign painting and people read his signs and they are influenced by what they read, so he does have a great influence on the world. So lets be very careful how we teach our kids and let them know how important they are as individuals, and that they are important to God too, as individuals, and let them realize that as they grow up and become men and women.

FARM LIVING WAS THE LIFE FOR ME!

MY EARLIER DAYS of living on the farm were very important. Farming is what the majority of the people depended on for their livelihood. There were many farms dotting the country side and farmers had no other way of making a living except by farming and it is a very important part of our heritage that we remember. I was born and raised on a farm. I used to be the water boy when I got old enough to carry water to the field, they liked fresh water occasionally. Before then, my world was pretty small. It was just inside the house. I was real young and didn't venture out. I don't remember much about that, then I finally got out in the yard and played in the sand. I had my own garden and I liked to see things come up and grow. I guess, that's the reason people made farmers, from necessity and also like to grow things, to see them come up from a seed, fertilize it, cultivate it and see it make corn, cotton, food, peas and so-forth. So I guess that's the reason a lot of people enjoy farming. It is so much different today from what it was then, because we now have large farms, all of the small farms have gone out of existence. We depended altogether for our livelihood. On our farm we had cows, hogs, mules, and chickens. We depended on the cows for milk and butter. We had chickens for eggs and also for cooking. We depended on our garden for vegetables that we would have for dinner, and our corn that we grew to feed the hogs and cows and also to make meal to feed the chickens.

A BITE OF SOMETHING SWEET

. . .

ON THE FARM we depended a whole lot on the crops we grew and the garden we had for food. We were unable to buy too much food and we always had a cow or two. We had a lot where we kept the mules and inside of that lot, on one side of the barn, (the barn had two sheds) the biggest barn was in the middle where the mule stayed. The shed on the side was the cow pen (we called it).

BOOGERS!

OFTEN TIMES I went to the cow pen with my mother in the afternoon, to watch her milk. I was just a small child, big enough to climb a gate and get up on top of a big post that was the gate post and did a little daydreaming or fascinating or something as she milked the cows.

I WOULD LOOK off into the west where the sun was just going behind the trees. It was beautiful, and I wondered what was over there, where the sun went, because I had not gotten old enough to really know too much about the workings of the days, the sun, the night, and the moon, etc. And then I would look across the field that had a lot of stumps left from the big pine trees that they cut and had rotted and they never would rot because they were solid. They were like some animals standing out there. Then to one hillside was a giant tree that was dead that lightning had struck several times. It had died but it still had limbs. The sun reflected off of it. It looked like a pretty friendly creature at that time, but as I sat on top of the gatepost waiting for my mother to get through milking and dark finally fell at dusk and all these thoughts and things in the field became "boogers", as we called them, something that would "get ya'"; expect them to come out and grab you. Then, the old, big tree on the hill that as darkness and dusk began to dim, then it looked like some great big creature with it's arms outstretched- it might grab you and take you away.

So, I was glad when my mother got through milkin'. She had to milk the cow, take the calf and let it sit a little bit and then tie it back off so that way she could get the cow to give the cream, and that was an important part of the milk, to get the cream and she would not do that. She thought she would hold it up and save it for the calf, cause she let the calf in for a while to get what milk she could. At night she had to separate them or he would get all the milk.

As MOTHER GOT through we would go in the house after it got dark. It was a humble home with kerosene lights and wood fireplace and no electricity. But when I got inside I felt safe and serene and a sense of security because I was at home with my mother and father and my sisters. This was a great feeling, one I had when I left the top of the gate post because I thought some "boogers" or some tree or big old creature was gonna grab me before I got in the house. So, home, even as humble as that one was, was a place of refuge and a lot of serenity.

BEING A MOTHER --THE BITTER PART OF THE BITTERSWEET MEMORIES

. . .

A BITE OF SOMETHING SWEET

Having to talk like this, it's kinda hard to say all the things about certain subjects at one time, so you think of something that you should have said that should have been someplace earlier in the tape. And the subject about life and babies, back there somewhere near the beginning, I should have mentioned that women and mothers don't get the recognition that they should. I suppose we might refer to their role or part of their role in childbearing as the bitter part of the bittersweet mysteries of life, in God's plan that they would be the one to bare children. They have to go through nine months of discomfort and sometimes some of them are sick all the time and then at the end of that, they have to have the pain and travail of childbirth and then when the child is born, it has to take it's daddy's name. The mother has already given up her maiden name and she has to take her husband's name, in most cases. Then the daddy gets to pass our the cigars and brag about the boy or the girl that he has. The mother is proud of her child and she loves it, so I think that they are the ones that should be recognized more fully for helping reproduce the world and also for their loving care of these children once they are born.

I thought that I had the most wonderful mother in the world. She always took care of me and saw to my every need when I was sick. Day or night, she was right there, laying her cool hand on my brow or to doctor my ailments or whatever it might be. If I made a good daddy for my children, I have to give my mother credit because of her attitude and her love and kindness toward me when I grew up. I suppose that my daddy loved me but he was pretty busy trying to make a living and worrying about were the next meal was coming from and clothes, and so-forth, so I guess maybe he didn't have too much time to spend with me, however, I think he loved me.

. . .

BRUCE HENNIGAN

FARMING AND LOG ROLLING

ON THE FARM, which has been almost seventy years ago, that I was raised on, the only thing between the farmer and starvation, in most cases, was two mules, a Studibaker wagon, and a couple of George's plow stock, maybe a steel beam breaking plow and the middle buster. These were pretty essential to the farmer in those days if he could financially afford them. Some people could not afford to have these different instruments. They had to borrow from somebody else if they needed any of them. Sometimes a wagon or plow. And also if you had a cotton planter that planted cotton and a fertilizer to put out the fertilizer, and these were pretty important pieces of equipment.

THE FIRST THING was to prepare your ground. In February you start to clean it off. You had to cut your corn stalks and knock the cotton stalks down from the previous year, cut all the bushes that came up, pile 'em up and burn 'em. You had to pick up the roots and anything of that matter and sometimes try to burn out an old stubborn stump or two that was in your way for farmin'. The place that we lived on was 120 acres and about 40 or 50 acres of open land. It was suitable for farmin'.

IT WAS customary for the farmer to clear a little bit of land each year for cultivation. That means getting all the brush and the trees off of it so he could plow it up and plant it. It was "trash" ground, they called it, which would produce much better than the older ground. It was a lot more difficult to work because of the stumps and the roots. They had to cut down the big trees and saw 'em up in about 8 or 10 foot lengths and get a log rolling.

. . .

AT A LOG ROLLING, we would invite all the neighbors in and they would pile logs up in piles and burn them. They would use a stick about 8 or 10 feet long and would slip it under the log with a man on each end. They would take about six loads to the log to pile them up and burn them. Then, you had to go around and be sure that the logs were burned before you could plow the land. The women would be at home fixing a big dinner of fried chicken, chocolate pie, or any kind of vegetables that you wanted and maybe a potato pie, pumpkin pie or whatever and they would have a real feast at noon when you came in.

BACK IN THOSE days farming was serious business. It was the livelihood for hundreds of families. Those small farms dotted throughout the country. Each farm jutted up against another farm. These farmers had to try to make a living solely on farming, which was rather hard to do. First, you prepared your ground for your crop.

CORN WAS USUALLY the first to be planted, you planted it about 3 feet apart and covered it, and then, when you start to cultivate it, you would get on top of the middle left and you made the deep part to plant it in and plowed it down toward the corn. The cotton was planted on top of the furrow that was put there by the middle buster. Sometimes you ran your middle buster over your land, break up the land, and put our the fertilizer and throw your dirt back on it and then come along and use a "sweep" and a "scooter", which would open up a little trough for you to plant your cotton in. The planter had a wheel on it and had little drivers on either side that ran back to a "hopper" that held your cotton seed and in that "hopper" was a blade that had holes in it. The rods that came from that wheel in front turned that plate around and each time it came to the hole where the spout was that went down to the ground, it dropped cotton into that little furrow. And then you had a wheel behind it that plowed on either side of it that would put a little dirt back on the cotton and the wheel packed it down.

USUALLY, you planted your corn in March and your cotton in April and May. Cotton was more of a warm weather crop than corn was. It took warm weather for it to grow. You had to depend on the weather, whether you got enough rain, too much rain or what, to make your crop. It was a big gamble for all of the farmers and they put all they had into the fertilize and seed-feed and so-forth. It was very important to get the right season.

THE FARMER always had to depend on the elements for rain for his crop, whether it was going to make it or whether it was going to be dry and burn up. If it was dry and your crop didn't get enough rain, you would be in bad shape financially for the next year because you had to gather your cotton crop in the fall of the year and take it and get it "ginned", turn it over to the man where you bought all of your groceries and your feed and the fertilizer that it took to make the crop. Sometimes you would have some money left over and sometimes you would still owe him money, and you would have to carry on until the next year or so.

FARMING WAS A VERY difficult thing in the sand hills of Louisiana and I'm sure it was the same way in other parts of the country, so it was serious business for the farmer, whether he would be able to make a crop to feed and clothe his family. It is quite different from what it is today. We're on a fixed salary and we know where our next dollar is coming from and we know how to plan to make arrangements that we might be able to have what necessities of life and a few other things that we enjoy.

THOSE FANTASTIC MEN IN THEIR FANTASTIC MACHINES

WHEN I WAS A YOUNG CHILD, old enough to be able to notice things, there were very few automobiles. I hardly ever saw one at all. Some people had buggies that carried two people and one little rumble seat in the back that you could probably ride in. It was kind of a light vehicle that one horse could pull and used a wagon that took two mules to pull it. For a lot of people that was the only type of transportation they had to go to town to go to church, or anyplace.

I SAW my first airplane when I was about 5 or 6 years old over at my cousin's house. We didn't have an automobile. I believe it was on a Sunday afternoon. I had been hearing about airplanes but I had never seen one. It came over Red Hill from the south. We heard it coming. Mother and Daddy said "I believe that's an airplane", and sure enough it came over the hill and you could see that it was a small plane. It was quite an exciting time and I got to see my first airplane.

Now I THINK BACK to that first airplane and think about the jet planes that we have to day, and about the rocket ships, and all of that going to the moon and orbiting the earth, walking on the moon and going into outer space and exploring other planets.

It's a different world and a great step forward. Nobody at that time envisioned or even thought of the change that would take place. A few scientist predicted it but nobody believed it, so, I see what a change has been made in my lifetime, which I think is fantastic. I thank the Lord that I have lived to see it and enjoy some of it because I was really interested in space and airplanes, and so-forth, so it is really quite a change for an old country boy walkin' down a sandy road and seeing his first airplane. The rocket ships and airplanes of today go across the country in a matter of hours.

THE LORD'S BLESSINGS

I DON'T THINK I can stress how important the farmer was in that day, and there was lots of 'em. Small farmers. They are a part of our history and a part of our heritage. Many important people came off the farms of that time, preachers, some lawyers and doctors and I'm sure that most of our friends that were farmers and it was a serious business and sometimes we don't like to listen to what happened when we were young, but if we do talk about it, it's not to remind someone that they should be thankful for what they had and we had it so hard when we were growin' up, but it is a part of our heritage and we should be thankful that God has blessed us down through the years like he has.

ONE OF THE blessings from the Lord and I'm thankful for that and my family, that I came from a barefooted country boy to here and I have a reasonable amount of money, comfortable home, and plenty to eat and plenty of love from my family. I have around me, my children and my grandchildren. I don't think there is anybody anymore luckier than I am.

COTTON PICKING TIME

MONEY WAS a problem in those days, there just wasn't any money to be had, so you pawned your land hopin' you would make enough money to pay your debts for that year and furnish maybe each child with a pair of shoes and maybe two pair of pants and two shirts, so that they might go to school and church.

As YOU PLANTED cotton and corn you waited for it to get big enough to cultivate it, keep the weeds and grass out of it, fertilize it to keep it growing. The cotton would be the first thing as it came off. You would have to chop it, thin it, with it hoe, keep the grass and wheat out of it when it got up knee high and then about the 4th of July you get to lay by. After that you would cultivate it, wouldn't have to plow it anymore. The corn was usually ready by the time the cotton was and that was somethin' to look forward to because we didn't have much work to do until the cotton started opening again in August and September.

YOU ALWAYS HOPED that you made a lot of cotton but you hated to have to pick a whole lot of it. To pick it you would pull the sack behind the straps on your shoulder until it got so heavy that you couldn't pull it, then you carried it and weighed it and emptied it up and came back for another round. After you had a bale of it, you would take it to the gin and get it ginned.

. . .

I ALWAYS LIKED to go to the gin and watch the gin work. I'd get the one with the shed or had the suction pipe that sucked them things down. That was quite a deal for a young boy like me. And you would have to take your cotton when you baled it up and you had to carry it over and set it until they had some cotton buyers around.

CHOPPIN' cotton was kinda hard work. You had to have your cotton about 6 or 8 inches apart after you got all the grass around it and then if the sand was kinda hot it would burn your feet and you were glad when the cotton got big enough to have shade so you could walk in the shade. You had to be careful not to step in bullnettle. We had bullnettle down there that would sting real bad if you stepped in them. Sometimes, somebody would slip one over in your side of the road just so you would step on it. It was kinda mean to do that but that we the kind of trick that they would pull on you.

MY MOTHER WOULD GET up and cook breakfast, milk the cows, wash the dishes and then get everything for dinner and then she would come to the field at about 9:00. She would help us chop cotton or pick cotton until about 10 or 10:30. Then she would go to the house and cook dinner. Not all mothers did that, but my mother was a very industrious type of person. She liked to always be workin' and helpin' out so she really did her part on the farm to help us when we were farmin'.

WE ALSO PLANTED A GARDEN. That was about the first thing. We had to have a garden and planted one when the earliest frost was over so we would have vegetables; mashed potatoes, English peas, turnip greens, onions, snap beans, all of those things to eat as early as possible so we would have something to supplement our food that we had to eat, and a garden was a pretty important part of farming.

IT WAS good if you had a garden that you could eat out of until about the middle of the summer. We planted peas to eat also, in the field. That was an important part, peas and corn bread. And then at suppertime we had cornbread and milk that was left over from dinner, if it didn't ruin, because we didn't have refrigeration or ice or anything for quite some time. Finally, we had an ice man and got an ice refrigerator, to keep our milk cold. Up until then, if you wanted cold milk you had to put it in the well. You had to let it down with a rope and be careful not to turn it over. When you went to get water out of the well, you would draw the water out with a bucket and if you turned that milk over you would have to wash the well out and draw all of the water out several times to get all of the milk out.

THE HOUSE

LIFE on the farm was the only way a lot of people had to make a living. I don't remember too much about the earlier days. We moved to a house in Saline that was made out of rough lumber; planks that were an inch thick and twelve inches wide and about 8 feet long. The planks were nailed vertical to the 2 X 4's. There was a brace through the middle of the boards to keep them from falling. We didn't have regular studs, except they had some for the doors and windows. They used braces in the culverts, then where the number 12 planks were nailed together before stripping the metal with cracks, hopefully it would hide the crack and keep the wind and the rain out.

THE FLOOR, or fireplace room, which was made of clay, was sealed with tongue and groove boards, which had a little slot for another tongue to fit into it and made it air tight. The ceiling was sealed with some of the same type of material.

I WAS in the fireplace room, or the family room, with two beds in there and some chairs; maybe a couple of rockin' chairs for momma and daddy and we had to sit in straight chairs around the fireplace in the winter time. Of course, we had to have a pretty good fire and people had to wear a good many clothes to stay warm because our house was not very tight.

IN ANOTHER ROOM, the big room, a bedroom; the floor was made by 1 x 12 planks that didn't have a tongue and groove. It wasn't sealed and you could see though the cracks in the floor. There were two beds in there for my sisters to sleep in and any guest we had to come along. I can't see for the life of me why anybody would build a house with cracks big enough to stick your finger in and freeze to death in the winter time. If I didn't have so many quilts on, it was frosty enough in there, I would have so many on I couldn't turn over. On the north side was a kind of a lean-to extension of the room of the main part of the house that wasn't sealed. You could see the raw boards up there and what came down to the walls on the outside was cracks there for the wind to blow through.

. . .

WE NEVER DID HAVE a glass window in that room, there was always a wooden shutter, which was the custom in that day if you didn't have a good bit of money to buy glass windows you would have wooden shutters. This house had wooden shutters when we moved into it, even in the living quarters. They didn't have any lights and you would have to open the wooden shutters and in the winter time the wind would come in and be pretty cold.

I REMEMBER when my uncles came out and put in some glass windows. We thought we was gettin' up-town when we had glass windows. I remember the first time that I remember anything about them in that house is that I went to the door and got a hold to the knob and I wanted to go home. I wanted to go back to the old place. That I was tired of that place.

WELL, I didn't get to go back home until I was around 3 years old, I guess, and the roof of the house was made out of boards. You had to go out in the woods and get either a Cypress tree or a Pine tree and cut it in blocks by 2 1/2 feet long. The trees in those days were virgin pine if you could find one that had the big heart in it and the heart tender would not rot like the sappy part of the smaller trees. You would have to take 'em and split 'em up in pieces of about 4 or 6 inches wide and then use a mallet to line the boards out. You would just start about a quarter of an inch thick and then hit it with your mallet and the wood was split real good and then you would come out with a board about 4 inches wide and 2 1/2 feet long. Sometimes it would be 6 inches wide, depending on how wide you wanted to make 'em. Then you would have to put rafters and cross pieces on them and nail these wooden boards onto the top of a house and know how to do it to keep it from laying through the cracks, cause you had to overlap each one to keep the cracks showing, to keep it from rainin' in. Sometimes it would leak a little bit.

You would have to give a house-covering, to let your neighbors know when you wanted to cover your house so they would all come and help cover your house in a day. Some of them claimed to be experts so you didn't have any problem getting good advice when you went to cover your house up. All in all it was a pretty rustic house. It was pretty cold in the winter time, and it was a little bit cooler in the summer, I guess because you would get so much air in that house. In one of those lean-to's was a kitchen stove and a dining room. It just had a table and a wooden stove.

For the wooden stove, we had to go out and cut down pine trees and cut off blocks and split 'em into about 2 inch square sticks and let 'em dry so they would burn real good and quick. When you got up in the morning to cook breakfast you might get your breakfast a lot quicker if you had a dry stove to start off with 'cause it would take a long time to get wet wood or green wood to start burning. It made good food but it was sometimes a lot of trouble to get the thing goin' right and hot enough to cook, but that is what we used for cookin' our food until we moved to Shreveport in 1942.

THE WAR TO END ALL WARS

I remember when World War I ended in 1918. We had no way of knowing about the war ending except by community telephone. Somehow, somebody heard it. There were no radio's at all. Newspapers, once a day got through the post office. Word spread that the war ended. You could hear guns shootin'. People hollerin' all over the country side. I remember we had one big ole saw mill saw that was about 3 or 4 feet across hangin' across the shed and I went out there and beat on it and you could hear people beatin' all over the country, tires, plows and everything they could find to make noise because the war was over. I can just barely remember that.

THE WATER BOY

YOU HAD to be about 7 or 8 years old before you could take much responsibility of workin' on the farm. You had to be the water boy, I did. I had to carry water to my sisters, my brother and my dad. They liked a fresh drink of water out of the well and two or three times more in the afternoon. It would be my job to carry it to 'em and sometimes I wouldn't get there quick enough and they would come and rake me over the coals. Then, eventually I got to where I could pick cotton or chop cotton. Then I had to do that. They would brag on me and I would really work hard to pick a lot of cotton or chop a lot of cotton.

OF COURSE, IN CHOPPIN' cotton, that's when you had to thin it and get all the grass out of it. Corn was the first thing that you really planted and you had to plant it by hand and drop each grain separate. Then, after the corn came up you had to plant your cotton. The cotton came later and we would hope that it wouldn't come a big rain on it and pack the ground where it would come up. Of course, after the corn and cotton came up it was cultivating time. You had to cultivate it to keep the grass out of it and thin the corn out with the hoe and keep the middles plowed out.

EVENTUALLY YOU WOULD QUIT PLOWING it that it would make and you would do the cotton the same way. Some summers, the season wasn't any good and your corn would burn up and you wouldn't have any corn to feed through the winter, to feed your horses, mules or hogs. They depended on corn for feed. Sometimes you would pull corn leaves off, hang it up on the corn stalk after the ears matured and let 'em dry out. In the after noon you would go out and tie 'em up in bundles and let it dry until the next day and then you would go out, haul it in, put it in the lofts, and feed it to the horses, mules during the winter months.

AND THEN, the cotton, it wouldn't be ready to pick until about the later part of August and right before we started school we would start pickin' cotton. School always got in the way of farmers because the children couldn't help much when they went to school except when they got older, in the afternoon, they would pick cotton. First, you would have to chop it. In early August and September was still hot, but there wasn't much to do when you got home after school and sometimes when things got real bad you had to stay out of school work, pick cotton or farm, help do anything that your daddy needed to be done and couldn't do all by himself.

CUTTING SPROUTS AND OTHER BUSY WORK

. . .

IN FEBRUARY you would have to go out and cut the bushes off the land you planted on, 'cause they would grow up during the summer pretty big and you would have to go out and cut those bushes. We called them sprouts. You had to pile 'em up, burn 'em and then that new grass I was talkin' about, where they had the log rollin' and it was cultivated.

THE BUSHES COME UP ALMOST solid so you had to cut those bushes down when you went to cultivate it so the stuff would make. There was always something to do on the farm if you would do it. Some of it wasn't very pleasant to do. Even when it rained it seemed like your daddy would always find something to do. Either pick off peanuts, shell corn or fill up the hole that washed out in the terraces or plow up a row of dirt to keep the water from washing your land. He made it in such a way to let the water drain off gradually.

IT SEEMED like my dad always found something to do so we worked from Monday until Saturday dinner. We would always have Saturday dinner till Monday morning off and we always looked forward to that. I guess that's the reason we could hold out during the week.

SWIMMING HOLES AND WATERMELONS

ON THE FIRST of July we laid all the stuff by and there wasn't very much work to do so we got to go swimming, fishing, and run around all over the country; playin' and doin' whatever we liked to do, swimmin'. We had a fine swimmin' hole, so it wasn't all bad.

. . .

WE WOULD FIND a watermelon patch to get into or a grapevine or somethin' of that nature. We would have a time eatin' grapes, watermelon and even sugar cane every once in a while.

WE HAD one Big Ditch we always liked to play in. It was about 20 feet deep. Kids from all over the country went out there to play in it and I think now what a thrill it was to play in the Big Ditch and then I go lookin' down the Grand Canyon and I'm all inspired, can't find words to express how you feel from lookin' from the big ditch and then lookin' down Grand Canyon. Little did I realize that when I played in the Big Ditch that I'd ever get to see the Grand Canyon first hand. I had read about it in books, but seeing it first hand was quite a thrill and something I will never forget.

SOME YEARS we planted sugar cane on the farm and it was a kind of a cane that grew up tall but it was sweet and we made syrup out of it sometime. Earlier in the summer, before the sugar cane got ripe, it was real strong, but it was pretty good. With butter and biscuits you would be glad to get it.

CLAY CHIMNEYS

THERE WERE several different projects that farmers depended upon their neighbors for. I mentioned the covering of your house, and there was a chimney dobbin' that they would have. If a chimney had fallen down or had worn out, the neighbors would come in and help you build your chimney. You would

A BITE OF SOMETHING SWEET

have to get some clay for the building of the chimney. Most farmers had clay built chimneys because they weren't financially able to buy bricks.

IF YOU HAD A BRICK CHIMNEY, you were considered kind of rich. We never was that fortunate. We had to rely on a clay built chimney that would last about 8 or 10 years, depending on what kind of clay you got. Good clay would last longer. We would have to go up the red hill on the other side of our house. There was a lot of clay up there. We would dig up a bunch of it and haul it away to the house and then get enough of it to build a chimney and you would make you a ???? with a ? and a shelf running down from it and some sticks on it, kind of mix the clay up as it went through the barrel. It had a hole at the bottom shovel it out and put it in a wheelbarrow and haul it to a ? where you made you a "catch"? they call it, to build a good chimney.

YOU WOULD PUT dirt in the barrel and start to mix up by hookin' a mule to a beam that run over it and let him walk around and turn it. This makes your clay from the water. You feed your dry clay in at the top and keep enough water in there so it is the right mixture when it comes out the bottom. You had to go out in the field and pull up a bunch of crabgrass or long grass and bring it in and mix it in with the clay. Cats? they called them, were about 8 pounds a piece, so that the clay would stick together.

THERE WAS ALWAYS one expert in the country who always prided in his ability to build a good chimney. They usually called on him to be the builder. You would get you four poles and put 'em up as high as you wanted the chimney to the end of the house and then get you some sticks out of pine logs to go across to put your clay cats on. As you went up, you put a row of cats and stick and put another row of cats and then it was four sided, you make sure you get it good and tight where the fire wouldn't catch the house on fire when you had a fire in the fireplace.

So, it usually took a full day to build even when you had several people helping you. You would have a big dinner like you did at the log rollin'. When the chimney got built, you would have to get the expert to go inside and build you a firebox out of clay. He had to build you a box out of clay and pack it in behind it and let it dry pretty good before you burnt that box out. When you got ready to use your fireplace after it dried a while you would just build your fire in there and burn the wood and dry the thing out.

FOOD FROM THE FIREPLACE

THE FIREPLACE WAS A PRETTY important thing on the farm because it was the place where all the family met, especially in the winter months. We would sit around the fire and talk, keep warm. Naturally, it felt a little cozy and the flame and coals were kind of soothing to the nerves. You also got to visit with your family and talk about things. You could heat peanuts or you could put you some sweet potatoes in the ashes and let them roast.

MANY A TIME MOTHER pulled hot ashes out on the hearth and put the Dutch oven on it and put biscuits in that Dutch oven and put a big metal lid on top and put hot coals on top and make some real good biscuits. She would make cornbread the same way. It would be late in the evening and didn't want to build a fire in the stove. We'd have hot biscuits, butter and syrup or corn bread and milk for supper, which was pretty much the goin' in those days for supper, you didn't have too much but we enjoyed all of that.

SICKNESS

THEN, sometimes when you would get sick, at the beginning of the farming season, all of the farmers would gather round and plow up your land, rake your land, plant your corn all in one day and help you out if you were sick. I had that happen to me one time, where they came to my house one day and plowed up the ground and planted the corn. I appreciated that.

WHEN SOMEBODY GOT SICK, usually people would help out. They would sit up all night if need be with a sick person. They would do all they could. In those days we had a country doctor in town who would make house calls. We were fortunate to have two. When I was sick at eleven years of age; I had pneumonia in the winter time and we used Dr. Hailey, he wasn't too good. He was just kind of a nice doctor who did some nice talkin' and not too much doctoring. Then we had old Dr. Tate, who was sort of a wino, but he was a good doctor. He doctored on me after I had the pneumonia. I had it real bad.

AT THAT TIME, those who had pneumonia had to go through a crisis. I never could figure that out, but anyway I did go through crisis. I didn't know anything that was happening for quite a while and when I came to, I began to get better. I just had a lot of trouble with pneumonia in the lungs so this country doctor, Dr. Tate said "get you a cast iron kettle and get you some real hot coals and put it in the pan and set it by the bed and put water and pine knots, turpentine, and Vicks salve in that kettle and let it steam. Then get you a funnel and hold it over your mouth and nose and breath in the steam to cut that phlegm and stuff out, and it did.

BEFORE I GOT OVER THAT, I didn't have to go to school for the rest of the year because something happened to my left leg. It settled in my left leg. I don't know if it was a blood clot or not but I couldn't walk on it for a long time, and when spring came, I still couldn't walk on it very well. The old country doctor wanted to operate on me but my daddy wouldn't let him. To this day, that leg still ain't exactly right.

BEES IN MY BONNET

I REMEMBER ONE TIME, I liked bees and I had some swarms of bees and hives in the back yard. In the spring of the year I got out there in that big box to watch my bees and see if they would swarm. I knew if I had 'em to swarm, I'd have me another hive of bees. One day I was sittin' in the box and they started swarming and sometimes they get mad and they will fight ya' if they start swarmin'. They got in that box with me and I couldn't run, I had to crawl. I crawled out of that box; I was eleven years old and I was hollerin' "Momma, Momma, momma!"

. . .

A BITE OF SOMETHING SWEET

THEM BEES WERE AFTER ME. That was kinda funny to me. I remember that day well. I liked bees very much. I wanted to be a bee keeper, but I never did quite make it. I fooled with them a great deal but I didn't have enough money to be a bee keeper.

SUGAR CANE

ANOTHER INTERESTING THING TO ME, of course everything I'm talking about is pretty dull to people that never lived on a farm, but we planted sugar cane down in a kinda damp place. Of course, in the fall of the year, before frost, we would have to go and be sure we got our cane made into syrup before the frost. I would ruin if it froze. You would have to go down and strip it with a cane knife and then cut the top out as far up as it went, if it was blue, you knew it was blue ribbon cane and you knew you could cut the top out up about where the blue stopped.

I USED to like to go the cane mill with my daddy and load the cane on the wagon and haul it several miles over the hill to Mr. Davis' and Mr. Phillip's cane mill. We would get it ground up and made into syrup. I always liked to go when I was small, about five or six years old, because I would get to drink some of the cane juice and watch 'em make syrup.

THE CANE MILL had three metal rollers in it and it had a beam across the top of it. You would hook it to that and then go round and round and feed your cane in there and it would squeeze the juice out and it would run over to the pan where they were cookin' the syrup. It was a big, long pan about twelve feet long and about four feet wide and it had sections in it. It was sitting over a furnace that you would put fire it. You would start your raw juice off and let it cook. When you added more to it; up toward the end were the chimmney was, it would get done quicker, so you had to hold it back till you thought your syrup was ready at the top end, and then you could let more juice come in at the other end and gradually feed it till where it cooked till where it was thick, cause you had to cook the water out of it. It would then run off in syrup buckets and it took an expert to know how to cook that syrup where it would be good and thick. You didn't want it too thick and you didn't want it too thin. I remember one time when we were down at Mr. Harpers and they had moved a mill down there. They would skim that stuff off the top of that juice and then they called it skimmin' and put it in a barrel.

I WAS STANDING up against that barrel and a yellow jacket stung me on the hand; I was a young fellow and I was letting everybody around there know I got stung by a yellow jacket because I never had anything hurt me that bad. Some people let those skimmin's stay in that barrel while they fermented; it made kind of a liquor to make it drunk to drink. Some people drank it but not me. If a hog got a hold of it, they would drink it too and it would make them hogs drunk. Syrup was a pretty important part of the diet, especially in the fall and winter months, with biscuits and butter and syrup and bacon and sausage. It was a king's breakfast.

SYBIL

WHEN I WAS ABOUT ten or eleven years old my mother's sister died, Aunt Fanny. She had two daughters and they had to have some place for them to live. Their daddy had tuberculosis and he was off in El Paso, Texas and was serving time out there. My mother and daddy decided to take the youngest one, who was about five years old. Her name was Sybil Sullivan, to live with us.

At first I resented her a good bit because I felt like she was getting some of the attention that I ought to be gettin', so I guess I was jealous of her, but that didn't last too long. I am kind of ashamed that I made that statement because it did some tellin' on me. But later on we became good friends and like a sister-brother relationship. She was a good friend as I grew older. She lived with us about eleven or twelve years, till she finished school. We had a brother-sister relationship up until I got married in 1935 and then I kinda got away from her I guess, being newly married because you get too busy or too involved to pay too much attention. When she finished school she went to live with her sister and work at the paper mill. I kinda lost out on that relationship as an adopted sister because I've never been close to her since, like I did before. She left and went to live with her sister, so I kinda regret I didn't keep up the brother-sister relationship with her, because she was just like a sister.

SCHOOL DAYS

I didn't start school until I was seven years old. I was too big a baby and I hated to leave my mother. When I went to school, I would get homesick before the day was out and start complaining that I was sick and my head hurt and my stomach hurt. I had two sisters and a brother going to school down there but that didn't do me much good. I wanted my mother. I was too big a baby, I guess. But they would always send me down to Uncle Sammy's house and I didn't want to go to Uncle Sammy Higgins house. That was about the nastiest place I ever was in. Then they would pick me up after school and carry me on home. That didn't last too long and after the first year, I guess I got used to it and began to like school pretty good.

I WENT to school in a two story, wooden-framed building until about the 3rd or 4th grade then they built a nice, two-story, brick school building which we were all proud of. Then, I had pneumonia when I was about eleven years old and I missed out on the 4th grade, I believe it was, and didn't get to finish.

WHEN I STARTED BACK in the spring I had a first cousin who went to the teacher and asked him why couldn't I go onto the 5th grade and try, at least, to see if I could make it..so I did. I never did have to go back to the 4th grade. I enjoyed going to school pretty good. I had some teachers I liked real well and so that I didn't, but I don't remember too many exciting things that happened in school.

OF COURSE, I always had girlfriends, I had two or three. We would always have a Christmas tree at Christmas time and you would always get some little present and we enjoyed that.

I MADE a lot of friends when I got in high school. In my class there was about 15 or 16, I guess, and we were all pretty close. Some of the girls that I liked, especially one or two.

. . .

LENA WAS a grade or two behind me so I didn't know her very well. In the 11th grade I won the American Legion award, which I was very proud to do. It was given to an honor student for several different points he exceeded in and all-around student, so I was glad to be chosen that. One of my girlfriends got it the year before, she was the smartest, so that gave me the chance to get it in the 11th grade. I appreciated that.

ALSO, they asked me to give an address and they called it the Baccalaureate address, I guess, that I gave. I was pretty much in high cotton giving that address. I don't know if I forgot any of it or not; Aunt Ann Lee wrote it for me and I felt like I was pretty important to get to give the Baccalaureate address or whatever they called that. So, I got to do that and that was the highlight of my school life, I guess.

THE SCHOOL BUS

IN THE LATE 20's my daddy bought a school bus. It was a Model T Ford with an old tin body on it. We ran it a year or two and had to do a lot of work on it. We had to keep it up so it would haul the kids.

THEM MODEL T's were quite different from BMW's. They had a low gear and a high gear and a reverse controlled by some pedals. You would put the gas to it and push on that pedal and you were in low gear and pick up speed and then take your foot off the pedal and put the gas to it and you would be in high gear. It had a brake pedal and a reverse pedal. You had to mash that to put it in reverse. You had to be careful when you got out, sometimes you didn't have a battery in it and you had to get out and crank it with a crank. If you didn't watch it, it would run over you if you forgot to put the brake up. It would start off running away from you when it cranked. You had to be careful when you were cranking it or it would kick back some way or another and it would break your arm. Many people got their arm's broke. We kinda got tired of that.

My dad traded it off for a brand new Chevrolet truck. It had a real nice body built by the man across the creek, who was real nice. It didn't have any glass in the sides but it had glass in front. We were real proud of it.

JANITORS

My brother Shelly drove it and I was the janitor at the school in the morning, while he was the janitor all the time.

He drove the school bus in the morning and many times I had to find the steam bar to heat the building down in the basement, that was below ground level. There was always a bunch of boys coming around to the window and you could see them as they came around the building and came right over to the door and come down some steps. He would scare 'em with a shovel and rake it down the wall. So I decided one morning I saw 'em coming around and I got ready to rake my shovel down that wall and they would hear that noise and when it hit the bottom of the step, it was the principal of the school. He didn't say good-morning or how-you-do or what's going on or nothing. He just snorted a time or two, stood

A BITE OF SOMETHING SWEET

around a little bit and then left. I never did try to scare anybody else.

AT THAT TIME, before we got electricity, we had what they called a dynamo. It was a thing that you made electricity out of a whole bunch of clear lookin' containers on shelves with batteries. That's the way they kept those things charged, is that dynamo or alternator, so we would have lights for the school. We didn't have electricity at that time. It took a long time to get electricity in the 30's I guess. I don't rightly remember.

I HAD to sweep all the floors in the building. About 10 or 12, and clean up all the paper and stuff while he was gone. Sometime I didn't get it all done by the time he got back. The school bus gave us a good reputation and brought in a little money too, so we had it a little bit better that way. Farming was kinda hard goin' so we had a little extra money to buy things with then.

IT WAS QUITE different from the Studabaker wagon that my mother used to use about twice a week. She would put me in the wagon and I would go with her. I was just a tot then. We would go up to the saw mill about two miles up the road and she had a bunch of customers up there, white and black, that she sold milk, butter, eggs, chickens and all types of vegetables to. She was always trying to make extra money so she helped out a lot in that respect. We finally got rid of the Studabaker wagon and got a Model T car.

WHEN SHE LEARNED to drive that car we would always be glad that when she come back by the commissary cause you could stop in and get you a nickels worth of candy. That was about the only candy I would get for a whole week. You got a whole sack full for a nickel, and I had me one good time eatin' that candy.

I THINK this tape is just about ready to go off, so I'm gonna close out on it and come back later. It's kinda hard to tell anything exciting about your life that wasn't exciting. Some things, a few things were, but this wouldn't make a real best selling book, I know. But, there might be a few things that interest some people and they may find a few things on it that they might want to hear more about, I would be glad to tell 'em about it. If anybody hears it and I'm still around. I would explain to them......(end of tape).

CHAPTER 44

I found a spiral bound notebook after mother passed away. I had no idea she had hand written her life's story. Once again, it brought back to me the realization that my parents passed on to me one of the most precious of gifts: the gift of storytelling.

THE LIFE of Lena Elizabeth Caskey Hennigan
In Her own Words transcribed from her hand written notes found in a spiral notebook shortly after her death.

BORN AUGUST 29TH 1918 to Dossie Elmer Caskey and Minnie Lou Toms Caskey at Price's peach orchard which is between Bienville and Liberty Hill. In November of the same year we moved to Burk Place which is 6 miles north of Saline on highway 9. Daddy bought a large plantation at that time of 180 acres. The house was a big 2 story house with the kitchen in a room to itself out back of the house. This was where the black people who worked the place on halves cooked all the meals for the big house. We had almost 5 families of blacks that worked the place. Daddy bought all their food and clothes and gave them a house to live in and they gave him half of all they made on the farm.

AUNT SAVANNA DID THE COOKING. Uncle Dug Mobley, her husband, was the house man to run errands for Mama and Daddy. He also helped Aunt Savanna bring in wood and water. All of my family and Daddy's family tree is in our big Bible. My great great grandmother on my mother's side was a full blood Choctaw indian. Her name was Running Water. She marred a Clark and I believe my great grandmother named all of her children after the indians. My granddaddy was Tom Toms and his children were sample of the first -- Homer, Hunter, Walker, Minnie (my mother), Mary, Julia, and Lou Howard. A lot of the older children looked like indian but my generations were blonde. The indian came out in my children, expecially Ronald. My Daddy's family were Scot Irish and moved to Bienville parish from Alabama.

ABOUT THE TIME I was three years old, I remember a big black boy named Dink Lard whose job it was to tend to me. Lorraine (whose first name was Minnie) was the oldest child and was old enough to look after herself. But, Mary Lee who was the third child had polio when she was about 2 years old. She had a black girl to tend to her named Maybelle. We had a brother (the second child) who was burned in the groins when a coal of fire popped out on the blanket where he was sitting in a rocking chair. The burned place was about the size of a silver dollar but infection set in and there was no medicine that could cure it. His name was Johnny Elmer. He was 1 1/2 years old when he died.

NED (as she was known) was Julie Madeline and was a baby at the time the blacks tended to us and a girl by the name of Mary tended her. The blacks loved Daddy because he was good to them but the also feared him because he didn't put up with their drinking or running around on their wives. I remember him getting on his horse to ride over to the plantation and see if everyone was working and Moffus had not come home that Monday (his wife's name was Maybelle). So, Daddy went to another black's house on the Fair plantation and found Moffus and put a rope around his neck and brought him home and took him to the barn and threw the rope over a rafter and pulled him up just where he could reach the ground and whipped him. All of us kids were begging him not to kill Moffus. He didn't but he never run off from his family again!

WHEN I WAS ABOUT 5 years old they remodeled the big house and tore the upper floor off and put the kitchen in the house. About this time we all had measles and mumps and Mama had smallpox. The put her in the room across the hall from us. She also had a miscarriage when she had smallpox. Ned was about 2 at the time. The baby was a boy and Mama was about 6 1/2 months pregnant. Uncle Dug and Aunt Svanna took care of us and Uncle Dug made us some ice cream. Ned didn't eat all of hers and he finished it and took the measles from her.

THE SEPTEMBER after I was five, Mary Lee started to school and the let me start to take care of her. The last thing I heard from that time on until I married when I left the house was "take care of Mary Lee". We went to school in a one room school house and one teacher 1st and 2nd grade and then they built on 2 more rooms on the school and hired two more teachers. They roomed with us and we had one teacher that loved Ned and some one brought her (the teacher) an apple one day. She brought it home and gave it to Ned and she wouldn't give me a bite of it. The teacher wouldn't let her.

WHEN WE BOUGHT the first car in the community was the first cars any of most of us had ever seen. The first airplane that flew over scared everyone to death. The mules Daddy was plowing ran away from him pulling the plow. In my lifetime I saw the first car, airplane, radio, TV, refrigerator and such things as the atom bomb. Walk on the moon, satellites, cable TV, printer's press, you name it and it all happened first in my lifetime!

IN THE 1980's when the computer came I thought then I had seen everything. In 1991 I still don't know anything about them. Sean is 6 years old and knows more than I do. Now when I was about 5 years old, we had a phone but when it rang everybody's phone rang and everyone picked up and listened in on what was called the party line. Everyone knew all the gossip in the country. We went to church in the school house. Had a preacher once a month and of course everyone came to church in wagons and buggies and spent the entire day.

WHEN I WAS five we bought our first car, a Reo. It was a big car and had fenders on it. I ran out to see it and jumped up on the fender and fell off and broke my arm. Dr. Hailey in Saline put a splint on it and it healed that way. That summer we (the kids and Mama) had gone down to Aunt Belle's and Uncle John (Mama's brother) and when we got home Daddy was sitting on the steps holding his intestines in his arms. A cow had hooked him and ripped him open. If his dog (who was named Tip) had not caught the cow by the ear and held her head down so he could get off the horn it would have killed him. That was our first trip to Shreveport.

. . .

UNCLE RUFUS LANGFORD BROUGHT DADDY, Mama, Lorraine, Mary Lee, me and Ned all to the hospital. We had never seen a nun before and when we got to the Schumpert hospital and they came and got our Daddy, we all screamed and yelled for a long time. Uncle Rufus brought us and Mama back and left our Daddy over there with them women with the hoods on and we cried all the way home. When they went back to get Daddy out of the hospital I guess they were afraid we would embarrass them again!

. . .

DADDY BOUGHT a place in Saline right across from the school about a block off when I was in the fifth grade. He never sold the old place but he rented it out for the next 8 or 10 years until they moved back up there after Slayton and I had been married about 3 or 4 years. We moved to Saline on Thanksgiving day 1927 and the school burned that night. We had to go to school in an old store down town until the school was built back. The high school kids went to school in the church. When we moved back in the new school I was beginning the 6th grade. We all had to take the grade we were in over because we moved from a small school and hadn't learned as much as they had in the town school. Nothing much happened while I was in elementary school except every picture I had made I was wearing overalls. I loved to wear them all the time, striped overalls.

. . .

WHEN WE MOVED TO SALINE, we lived in a house between the railroad and the graveled highways during the depression. We had lots of hobos who came by asking for food and Mama never turned one away. She gave them something if it wasn't anything but a baked sweet potato or cold corn bread. My mother was one of the most giving persons I ever knew. No matter who came home with us from school or church she put a little extra water or milk in what she was cooking and had plenty for everyone. I never heard her complain one time about us bringing home company. When I was eleven years old we had revival meeting in a tent downtown and Brother Buchanan from Calvary Baptist Church in Shreveport was preaching fire and brimstone. I almost ran down the aisle to join along with 22 others, a lot of them adults. We were baptized in the swimming hole where we went everyday to swim but it was a holy place that day when all of us waded out and were baptized in it.

WHEN I WAS in the 9th grade Lorraine married Shelly and I fell in love with his brother, Slayton Hennigan. He thought I was a little girl and wouldn't have anything to do with me. His mother had to take his first cousin and raise her after Aunt Trannie died and so Sybil and I became good friends. I would go home with her and spend the night just so I could see Slayton. In May 1933 I started dating Pete Rogers but still loved Slayton. He was dating a girl named Vera Smith. Pete got his brother's car one night and me and Pete, Slayton and Vera went to a revival at Readhimer. Pete was driving so I couldn't watch Slayton and Vera in the back seat. On the way home we parked to talk and the preacher who was preaching the revival came along and stopped and Slayton told Pete to get out of here so he did. The next day in home economic class one of the girls began telling about her and the preacher coming home last night and saw someone stopped and the stopped to see if they needed help and they sped off. Needless to say my face got redder and redder. I got up and went in the cloakroom cause if anyone had looked at me they would have known who it was! That was my last and only time to ever park!

ABOUT THIS TIME we had a Jump Josey party every Saturday night at someone's house. It was like square dancing now. We always got to go but with no boys. Lorraine was to look out for us. We danced the floor out of a house one night and all the community went the next day and rebuilt it. When anyone needed a new chimney and fireplace all the people came to their house and built it out of clay and grass and mixed it and made paddies and stuck them together. The women quilted while the men worked. Everyone brought a covered dish and we served it outside on tables. We also met once a year and worked the graveyards and had dinner on the grounds as they called it. Everyone showed off their cooking.

ON MAY 6, 1934 Slayton asked me to go to Shreveport with him to a singing. He was driving the school bus at the time. In fact, he drove the bus 11 years before we moved to Shreveport. He was bringing a load of people to the singing at the Municipal Auditorium and asked me to go with him and Mama wouldn't let me go. I just knew he would never ask me again but he did and I dropped Pete with a thud! In 1977 Pete and his wife Eva Dee came to a memorial service at Saline and he and Slayton and Brother Clay were talking and he told Brother Clay he thought he was going to marry me back in 1934 and Slayton came along and shot him out of the saddle. Me and Eva Dee were standing there and it sure did embarrass me.

. . .

BACK BEFORE SLAYTON asked me for a date I would invite him to school parties and he would meet me there and leave me there. He finally decided I grew up I guess. We dated until the following November and he never had kissed me so one night I kissed him and ran in the house. He never had any trouble after that. I graduated from high school when I was 16 years old the eighth from the top of the class of 18. Julia Stewart was my best friend then. Sybil had left Slayton's home 2 years before to live with her sister Muriel who had married. Slayton graduated in 1933 and got the award for best al round boy in school. I was as thrilled as he was. I was 16 in 1935 and still going with Slayton. In July, our first cousin Wimpy (Winnfield Hill of Castor) and Ned decided they were going to take Slayton away from me. He had come home with me from church to eat dinner with us which he did almost ever Sunday. He kept flirting with them and made me mad so I run off and went off in the woods. Slayton left and went home. That night I flirted with Pete and get him to bring me home from church and was sure that Slayton saw us. We did all of our courting in church and school activities and Jump Josey parties. That was like square dancing today. Slayton came be on Monday morning as I was hanging out clothes and asked me if I was going to go with him or Pete. I said you I guess. He said "I'm going to Alexandria with a load of watermelons and when I get back we are going to get married." I said OK. He came back and carried another load of melons to Shreveport and went by and got our marriage license. Of Course he told them I was 18 years old so he could get them. We were to marry on the 27th of July at 4 P.M. Slayton went to get the preacher (who was filling in for our Pastor, Brother Buckner) to marry us and he said "Slayton, I'm not a licensed preacher" so we had to get the justice of the peace to come to our house and marry us. Julia Stewart, R. J. Alison were my first cousins and Guy Wafer was Slayton's best friend and stood up with us. R. J. is dead. Guy was killed in the service and Julia married my first cousin Wayne Toms one year to the day later. We spent the night at Mama's that night and all of my cousins that I didn't want to see came over and made ice cream and carried on for hours. Seemed like Slayton finally told everyone he was sick so we could go to bed.

S~LAYTON CARRIED~ or moved me to his Mother and Daddy's and she had a kitchen off back of the house she fixed up for us with a bedroom and put a kitchen in a little room next to it. We lived with them until October and moved over to a log cabin that sat where Homer Morgan's house is now. Slayton still drove the bus and made $15 a month plus farmed some. After a year over there, Slayton's daddy wanted us to move back in a little house below their house and help him farm so we did. I got pregnant after we had been married 15 months.

W~HEN I WAS~ pregnant with Ronald, I got in a tub (wash tub) and I couldn't get out of it. You see I weighed 135 when I married and weighed that until I got pregnant with Ronal and went to 175 and never got below it except on time when I went on a diet that Dr. McKay gave me pills for. I went to 167 after a diet of a year and got off the pills and diet and gained it back in 3 months! Anyway I took a bath in a washtub and got hung in it and Slayton was up on the hill plowing so I had to get out by myself and I couldn't so I turned the tub over by rocking it and then I had to scrub the floor. With all the other children I went to 200 pounds and over with Bruce the most. I went to 225 lbs. But none of my babies weighed over 8 1/2 pounds, all of them were between 8 and 8 1/2 lbs.

. . .

RONALD CHARLES WAS BORN at home June 18, 1937 and Dr. Joyner delivered him with Slayton up in the bed with me. Dr. Joyner charged $20 for delivering him. He was the prettiest baby you ever saw. His granny Hennigan said he was too pretty and we would never raise him, but we did. When he was 2 1/2 years old he would slip off and go to his Granny's house. We decided we needed a little blonde headed girl to go with Ronald so we ordered her. Gwendolyn Elizabeth was born June 8, 1940. She was the prettiest baby you ever saw.

SHE HAD blonde curls until she was about 6 years old and took impetigo in her hair and I had to cut it real short and it came back dark.

DURING THE SUMMER OF 1941, Slayton's mother and Daddy moved to Shreveport and rented a boarding house that was right behind the old Charity Hospital. In was on Murphy St. where city hall is now. (Charity is where LSU Medical Center is now.) She rented out beds for people who had people in the hospital for 25 cents a night. In the summer of 1941 we went over in the school bus and parked it in their back yard and Slayton looked for a job and we lived in the school bus. He got a job in a meat packing outfit (Wilson) and couldn't handle the half of cows. He weighed 125 lbs. so he went to the Acme freight and couldn't handle that so we came back to Saline in October and he bought a mule and we were going to farm again.

WE DONE WORSE than ever in the farming bit. So, the next summer we went back to Shreveport and he got on full time at the Post Office. Course, the World War II was going on. We moved to a big duplex house on Hope St. but we didn't stay there but about 2 months and we rented a house on Buckner St. It was a 3 bedroom and big screened in back porch and kitchen and bathroom. The bedrooms were real large. We had 2 beds in each bedroom. Rooms were hard to find and houses were almost impossible to find because everyone in the country towns were moving to Shreveport and working at the shell (ammunition) plant in Minden. We got the house for $35 a month.

NED AND DOROTHY DISON and Dorothy Rogers lived in one bedroom. Wimpy and Billie Hill lived in one bedroom for 3 or 4 months until the could find a place. Mary Lee lived with us until she married and until Albert was born about 3 years I guess. Brother and Jeanette stayed with us until they found a place. When somebody moved out, somebody else would come in. Annie Lee and Marvin lived with us 3 or 4 months. During all this time we took turns using the kitchen and we bought out first refrigerator, washing machine, and stove that ran on gas. All the time before this we had an ice box that you put ice in and a stove that used wood or coal oil. Ned and the Dorothys stayed years. They didn't move out. Ned drove a taxi and worked in a drugstore.

ABOUT 1944 SLAYTON got draft notice that he had to go into the Army. He got me and Ronald and Gwen ready to move back to Saline and even rented us a house and I got pregnant with Sue. The lowered the ages that had to go to 25 years and Daddy was 28 and also everyone in post office was working to get him deferred as his work was essential to the war -- getting mail out -- so finally, he was deferred. (Note: Daddy turned 28 in 1942 and this was the year the draft age maximum was lowered to 28.

But, Sue was born in 1945 so I believe Mother was getting these two years mixed up. Bruce)

DURING ALL THIS time sugar was rationed, gas was rationed, oh yes, we had bought us a car by then. At first when we moved on Buckner Slayton walked all the way to work. Buckner is right were KSLA is now, right below Schumpert Hospital. We lived on Buckner Street about 7 years. When Sue was born I walked up to the Schumpert myself. Course, Slayton was with me! I remember I was in a ward with 6 women when I had her. She was the prettiest baby you ever saw. She was born November 14th 1945. She cost us $600 hospital and doctor bill. Doctor Cole delivered her. Ronald and Gwen went to school at Line Avenue school. Gwen wasn't in school at the time of Sue's birth but there was plenty of people living with us to keep her and get Ronald off to school.

RONALD WAS LEFT handed and never could write or spell. He could read anything but couldn't spell. Mary Lee had James Alton and Albert Lee while living with us and then they moved to Homer, Louisiana. We decided we didn't want to raise our kids in town so when Sue was 3 years old we bought a home in Blanchard, Louisiana and moved back to the country. We got about a city block of land and a 3 bedroom and living room and kitchen for about $5000. Course we had an outside toilet and no running water. We had a well on the back porch. We remodeled the house and built on 2 rooms, a screened in porch and also a bathroom in the house and put in running water. When we got settled in Blanchard and Sue started to school I went to work at Sears downtown in the bedspread and sheets etc. dept. I worked there about 6 months and got a chance to drive a school bus from Blanchard to Shreveport for $75 a month.

A BITE OF SOMETHING SWEET

. . .

WHEN MAMA and Daddy lived at Burk Place (Hennigan) we stayed with them the night after Daddy Dan died and Ronald went hunting the next morning down to Red Bluff and he got lost and came out on the Castor Lucky highway. He had walked about 25 miles. someone picked him up and brought him to Daddy and we just did make it to the funeral on time. Ronald was 15 years old.

THE CADDO PARISH SCHOOL BOARD furnished the bus, gas, and kept the bus fixed if it broke down. All I had to do was drive it. I could write a book about things that happened while I was driving that bus. I drove one year to Shreveport and the next year I got a bus to Blanchard School and a raise to $90 a month. When I retired after 25 years I was making about $335 a month. I killed a 12 point buck with my bus.

RONALD RAISED mink when we moved to Blanchard. We raised vegetables. he made a bust of his mink but I enjoyed fooling with them. He also had a horse named Charlie. Charlie even ate mustard sandwiches. Ronald bought himself a muzzle loaded shotgun and put some powder in it and didn't have any pellets so he put a marble in it and shot it and it hit a telephone pole and it came back and hit him in the center of his forehead. He still has a scar. It like to scared Sue to death. She came screaming that Ronald had killed himself. Blood was pouring down his face.

SUE FELL on a coffee can and cut her arms when she was about 4 or 5 years old. We rushed her to the emergency room and they had to take about 8 or 10 stitches in it. She still has scars on her arm.

About this time he taught Sue to ride Charlie. Charlie had a hump on his back like a camel. It didn't bother Ronald and his best friend Bobby Osborne but Sue had trouble riding him. She went with Ronald and Bobby everywhere they went if the would let her. When Sue was 10 years old on her birthday we told them we thought we had ordered her a little brother. We didn't know for sure but the doctor said I might be in the change of life. It was a change all right! We thought we had our family but we didn't. I quit driving the bus at Christmas and Bruce was born June 13, 1955 on his daddy's 41st birthday. He tried to be born butt first and as he said he has been backwards ever since in some way. He was born after I was in labor about 24 hours and they didn't have any thing but ether then to give you. The nuns at Schumpert thought he just wouldn't come down where they could reach him. I went in at 11 o'clock Friday morning. He wasn't born until about 11 A.M. Saturday morning. Dr. McKay (Edwin) delivered him. He came in Saturday morning and found him trying come butt first and he got in the bed with me and turned him around and he was finally born.

He was the prettiest baby you ever saw!

All of my babies had a head full of black hair when they were born. that September I started back driving the bus and the teachers let Sue out early so she could come home and take care of Bruce. We lived within a block of the school so I could get there in a few minutes. Ronald and Gwen both went to Fair

Park High School at this time. Ronald graduated when Bruce was about a year old and Gwen got married to Kenneth Brehmer the following January. Gwen and Kenneth lived in Shreveport for a while but finally moved into an apartment at Mrs. Sally Bostwick. Ronald went to work for United Gas in September of the year he graduated and Gwen worked at Rubenstein's and then the next year at Mid Continent Steel where she still works.

WHEN SUE WASN'T TENDING Bruce she was following Ronald and Bobby Osborne. When Bruce was 3 years old we moved out to the Rosenblath place. We bought 62 acres and a big house and 2 rent houses and a garage apartment. We got it all for $28000 at the time. Our payments were $275 a month and the rent on the houses helped to make the payment. We bought a herd of 11 heifers and Myrtle gave us a bull white face hereford. Myrtle also gave Sue a horse. We went to Mississippi and brought the bull and Babe back in a horse trailer. We lost 3 cows and 3 calves the first year. They died trying to have their calves. Course we never did make any money of the. We bought a cow also from the Osbornes and she tore the barn almost down to get away. We finally sold her too after catching her.

SUE WENT to work for SWEPCO and Wayne was her boss. She bought herself a Volkswagen and Wayne came out to do something on it and met her family. Get her to tell you his reaction!

OH, I'll have to tell you about the pig we raised in the garage. Bruce sure did like to go out and slop him. He loved it. We rented the garage apartment to Jean and Lloyd Burrows. Then Ronald used it for a taxidermist ship. They lived in one of the rent houses. Oh yes, he married Gloria Newman the first year we moved out there and lived there until we sold the place. Gwen lived in the other rent house until Rhonda was born. Then, she moved to Shreveport.

EVELYN CRAWFORD WORKED for us for 8 years tending to Bruce, Keith, and Kevin after Sue started to school at Fair Park. Ronald and Gil Lawton had lots of adventures together. they put a terrapin in a pressure cooker because he wouldn't open up. They set it on the fire and it blew up and got terrapin all over the ceiling of Mrs. Lawton's kitchen. She made them clean it up. They also made gunpowder and put it in stumps and blew them up. It's a wonder they didn't get killed.

DURING THIS TIME Slayton led the singing in Blanchard Baptist Church and Mildred Crowe Baptist Church. We went to Mildred Crowe about the time Bruce was 3 years old and Slayton led the singing for 12 years there. 6 years for Brother Lawton and 6 years for Brother E. Leo Palmer. The preacher at every church he led singing was our best friends, too. We had lots of adventures with all the preachers and really loved them all.

RONALD AND GLORIA moved out in one of the rent houses and had all their children there. Ronny, Randy, and Lisa. They lived there until we sold the place and we moved into a trailer in Bossier City when I was 55 years old and retired from driving the bus.

. . .

A BITE OF SOMETHING SWEET

GWEN LIVED in one of the rent houses until all her kids were born, Keith, Kevin, and Rhonda. She married Ronnie Ennis and moved to Shreveport when Rhonda was 9 months old.

SUE married Wayne Hammack and moved to Bossier City. They had Veronica about 7 years of marriage. Then Erik. They have lived in Bossier all their married life.

BRUCE MARRIED SHERRY KIDD. They had Sean and Casey.

WE LIVED in Saline when they married and left the trailer in Bossier for him to live in and go to school. We came back at least once a week to see Bruce and get him some groceries (This was during college and medical school before he met Sherry). He got a scholarship of some money and he got him his first car. He had one wreck coming from Blanchard to LSU after the first year of driving. He wanted us to move to Bossier.

(BRUCE: I never wanted Mother and Daddy to move to Bossier. I distinctly remember telling Daddy that I would NEVER leave Blanchard when I found out he was selling the land. Daddy and Mother decided to move a trailer to Bossier City so it would be someplace they could come back to from Saline and would allow me to live closer to LSU Shreveport. I was against the move from day one. But, after driving to LSUS 45 minutes one way twice a day, I was ready to move closer to LSUS.)

HE HAD SAID he would never leave Blanchard but after driving in that traffic for a year, he was ready to move. So we sold the place in Blanchard and moved to Bossier in a mobile home.

I HAD to retire from driving the school bus because my blood pressure got too high and I retired at 55 years of age but couldn't get my pension until I was 60. So I had to pay my retirement in until then. I started the pension with almost as much money as I was making driving the bus. We lived in Bossier from 1975 until 1977 when Slayton retired and we moved to Saline and stayed about 10 years. He led the singing in Magnolia Church for about 8 years. We sold our place in Saline and moved back to Bossier. After Bruce met and married Sherry Kidd and she was perfect for him and us. She still is a good daughter-in-law. Bruce finished his schooling and interning and they had Sean and Casey and bought a house in Chase Crossing and still live there at this time. All of our kids are the best and we love them so much and have had such a wonderful life it scares us.

BRUCE LIVED in the trailer in Bossier until he married Sherry. We moved there when he had been in college about a year in December, 1973. Daddy and I built a house on the lake in Saline. We bought two acres on the lake. (Mother and Daddy actually bought a mobile home and then added a long room with a living room, dining room, bathroom, and bedroom and a huge porch.) We lived there about 10 years before we sold the place to Dr. McInnis and bought a 16 foot wide trailer and moved it in the place in Bossier. We enjoyed the years in Saline. Slayton led the singing in Magnolia Baptist Church for about 8 years until he developed a cough and couldn't sing anymore. We lived in the trailer for about 3 years and then bought a home on

Poinsettia November 13, 1989. Here we sit. I piece quilts and Daddy piddles when he feels like it.

February 5, 1991 -- I am piecing on my 63rd quilt and in my blue book are who I made them for.

1998 -- At this time our family is as follows -- can't write at 80 years old.

Ronald and Gloria
    Ronnie and Debi -- Justin, Deanna, Debi children and his, Hollis Ann and Courtney Tyler
    Randy and Barbara -- Jordan Lee and Blake
    Lisa and Mark
    Gwen and Ronnie's kids together
    Keith and Dianne -- Kristi, Erin, and Kasey
    Kevin and Brenda -- Dustin, Corey, Nathan
    Rhonda -- Keinen and Brittany and Kyler
    Michael and Melanie, Larin, Mac
    Ronald and Liz -- Sarah
    Sue and Wayne -- Veronica and Erik
    Veronica and Chad -- Savannah, Jeffrey and Ashley
    Bruce and Sherry -- Sean and Casey

We adopted Shine Kidd when Junior died and never have had such a good friend.
    51 from me and Slayton and counting!

CHAPTER 45

I had not checked on my sister, Gwen in a couple of weeks. Gwen had experienced some serious medical issues about two years before. She ended up in the hospital with diverticulitis and subsequently had many complications. For months, she was in and out of the hospital and then in and out of various nursing homes for rehabilitation. I won't share the painful details. But she ended up at her grandson's house. Dustin and his family converted a room in their house to the best care center Gwen could possibly have. They got a hospital bed and put her favorite channel, the Game Show Channel, on her television 24/7. Our hope and prayer was she would recover. Her illness had abated after surgery but she never had the stamina or, possibly, the desire to get out of the bed and walk again.

My sister, Sue, recovering from her stroke, would often stay with us while her daughter and family went on vacation. We would take her to see Gwen and Sue would ask her to get up and walk. But, I think Gwen was just "comfortable" and happy where she was.

My daughter's best friend, Sarah Sutton, was getting married the Monday before Thanksgiving, 2026. Her father, Mark Sutton, my former pastor, best friend, and co-author was essentially home bound and living in Daytona Beach, Florida. Mark had received a lung transplant almost 9 years before and had gone into rejection several months before. There was no way he and Donna could attend Sarah's wedding.

I was shocked and honored when Sarah asked me to walk her down the aisle. When Mark's first wife (Sarah's mother) Susan became ill with ovarian cancer, Sarah stayed with us off and on for six years. She was more than Casey's friend. She was Casey's sister. I was so honored Sarah asked me to walk her down the aisle! I made sure it was okay with Mark and he said he was honored I would walk his daughter down the aisle.

I had visited Daytona Beach in August, 2026 to visit with Mark. I had been trying to go see him for a couple of months. We had a nice visit but he had fallen the night before and that turned out to be a downward turning point in his health. It was the last time I would see him. On New Year's Day, 2026 he called and wished us a Happy New Year. He sounds so happy and healthy. Three weeks later, he passed away.

So, back to Gwen. We had planned on heading south to Lafayette, Louisiana (a three hour drive) around noon on Sunday before the wedding the next day. God speaks to me in very subtle ways. I had this overwhelming need to go by and see Gwen. What is strange is that Sherry and Casey both, independently, said to check on her before we went out of town.

We went by to see her and I was shocked at her condition. She had deteriorated over the previous couple of days and was now unresponsive. As a physician, I knew what this meant. I knew she had days, if not hours.

When we got back into the car to head south, Casey lost it. She was VERY close to her Aunt Gwen. We had taken so many trips to Disney World with Sue and Gwen but for the past few trips, Sue had not been able to go. So, Casey had become Aunt Gwen's ride partner!

But, we agreed we would not mention it to Sarah. We did not want to ruin her day. That night around 11 P.M. my nephew, Keith, called to say Gwen was gone. We made it through the wedding and started home the evening after the wedding. I told Casey on the way home so she wouldn't be upset during the wedding. She was Sarah's maid of honor.

Gwen's family did not have a church home at that time. I realized I would have to be the one to handle the funeral. I asked my associate pastor, John Harp to be in charge. John knew Gwen and had visited with her in the hospital many times even though Gwen was not a church member. John ministered to her family often in those couple of years.

I spoke at Gwen's funeral. It was not as hard as I thought because I shared so may good and fond memories of my childhood and trips to Disney World.

Little did I know that in just a couple of months, I would be speaking at Mark Sutton's memorial.

In my next book, "Another Bite of Something Sweet" I will share more stories of Gwen and Mark Sutton. She is greatly missed. And so is Mark.

So, on 2026 Easter Sunday not only did I miss my sister, my friend, my father, and my mother but I thought of my brother in Christ, Gerald Brown and my biological brother, Ronald. One day, we will have a grand and glorious homecoming.

CHAPTER 46

ena Hennigan

My mother passed away in August, 2004. She went back into the hospital off and on throughout that summer. One of my greatest regrets came when my son, Sean, and I went to California for a church conference. We were at Disneyland and while on one of the rides, I got a phone call from my mother but I had no cell signal so it went to voicemail.

I did not know she had called and at this point in her illness, she was demented and did not know the time or day. She would have moments of lucidity. And this is what happened when she called. She left a voice message that was the most lucid and clear thinking she had experienced in months.

That voice message is long gone and when I heard it later on that day, I called her immediately. My sister, Sue, was staying with her at the time and my mother was once again disoriented. My special moment had passed. I wish I still had that message!

That July saw my parents' 69th anniversary. My wife, Sherry, was staying with her just a couple of days before and my mother had another moment of lucidity. She wanted to sign an anniversary card for my father. Sherry got a card and my mother wrote the sweetest note! And my father was upset that in all of the hospital visits my mother had lost her wedding ring. So Sherry got her another ring for my father and he put the ring on my mother's finger on their anniversary.

A couple of weeks later, she was gone. The night before my mother passed away, I stayed until about 9 PM. A sitter was coming to stay the night. At that moment, we did not expect my mother to pass away any time soon. She had gone into kidney failure and my father made the painful decision not to put her on dialysis. I told my mother good night when the sitter arrived. And I don't know why I said this:

"Mother, Ronald is coming tomorrow about 10 AM so you need to hold on long enough to tell him goodbye." My brother, Ronald was essentially home bound with severe COPD. He got a ride from his daughter and was there at 10 A.M. I got the call from my father about 1030 that my mother was gone!

I spoke at my mother's funeral. I did not wear a coat and tie. My mother loved my Hawaiian shirts so I wore her favorite one and I was able to speak at her funeral and share many of the stories from this book.

I may have already mentioned this, but many of the college kids who came to my mother's Sunday School class in the early 1970's came to her funeral. She was an extraordinary woman filled with love, laughter, and life.

For Easter, 2026, our church, Brookwood Baptist Church combined our contemporary and traditional music programs in both services. My daughter, Casey, has some issues with loud music because of her epilepsy. We sit outside the worship center at chairs and couches in the hallway centered around large screen TVs streaming the service.

The very first song really hit me hard. It was an older song, "Because He Lives". Two things grabbed me at once.

First, my good friend and former pastor and co-author, Mark Sutton, had passed away in January. This was the first Easter I did not receive a very special text message. Every Easter morning, my cell phone would chime and Mark Sutton sent me those priceless words, "He Is Risen!" To which I would reply, "He Is Risen Indeed!"

I had not received that message on this Easter morning. It hit me hard at that moment at the start of our Easter services.

Second, I thought of my mother and father. Mother had the most incredible clear alto voice. My father, being a tenor, often sang as I have mentioned in this book, as a "music director" in church. But mother would always join in. Her alto voice was spotless and she never hit the wrong note.

"Because He Lives" was one of their favorite duets, whether for church or just riding along in the car. On our long trips (at least for a child when an hour and half seemed almost a lifetime) from Blanchard to Saline, we didn't turn on the radio. No, Mother and Daddy sang. And, I sang along!

And so, sitting there realizing that Christ is Risen and my Mother, my Father, and my friend, Mark Sutton were sitting at the feet of the Risen Savior in heaven was a bittersweet moment. I cried and cried.

My mother always said she wouldn't die before Jesus came and as I have mentioned in this book, Jesus came for her. Jesus will come for all of us. Mother and Daddy both shared the "plan of salvation" so many times not only in Sunday School class where they both taught but also from the pulpit when they sand gave testimonies. I once heard it said that we will be shocked by who ISN'T in heaven and who IS. I know that on that Easter morning, the family I have lost and the friends I have lost is heaven's gain. One day I will join them. I hope you will, too.

CHAPTER 47

𝒲hen Daddy Gets to Heaven...

I SHARED the story of my father's funeral. But, there will have to be another book for what happened in the years between my mother passing away and my father passing.

After being married for 69 years, I was certain my father would grieve himself to death. That lasted for a couple of months. And then, this very different version of my father emerged. Stories for another time.

But before we get into those details, the Christmases! My father loved to sing "O Holy Night". When my mother was alive, he would always sing it at our annual family Christmas parties and my mother would sing along with her alto.

From as early as I could remember, my parents always had the entire family to their house on Christmas Eve. We would gather and eat candy and sandwiches and punch and then open presents in a wild, chaotic frenzy.

After my mother passed away, the party moved from their

house to my house. The first Christmas was tough. Daddy was still grieving and we all looked at the empty chair at the table and missed my mother. The loss was softened a bit. My mother had developed dementia before her last Christmas with us and she was slowly fading away. That was hard enough to deal with. But we knew she was in a better place in heaven playing Rook with all of my aunts and uncles who had passed on.

That Christmas, my father sang "Oh Holy Night" by himself. And at 90, his voice was as powerful as ever. There is a strange memory from that Christmas. My sister, Gwen's family had grown and grown. Mostly grandsons, but some grand daughters, all of her descendants had blonde hair. When they arrived at our house, the children were what my so n would call "feral cats" all playing and whirling and tumbling throughout our house.

In the midst of this chaos, the doorbell rang. I opened the doorbell and there standing on the threshold with a present in his hands was a blonde haired, blue eyed boy about seven.

"What are you doing outside?" I shouted above the loud din behind me. He peeked around me at the living room.

"Get in here. Now!" I said.

His eyes filled with fear and he shoved the present in my hands "This is from us next door. Please don't make me come in." And then he ran away as fast as he could. He was the child of one of our neighbors NOT one of my great-nephews!

In the years after, my Daddy would always tell us "these kids need name tags." And that wasn't a bad idea. His last Christmas with us, we had to move into a larger space and found a "lodge" on a local YMCA camp. It was rather rustic with a fireplace large enough to drive a van through. And that was the only heat!

Our family gathered with all the feral cats and their parents. My father once again, and for the last time, sang "O Holy Night". At the ripe old age of 97, his voice had not diminished in power in the years.

He passed away the following October as I have mentioned earlier in this book. When Christmas 2012 came that year, it was tough. We met at the church as the lodge was being demolished to make way for a shopping center.

Who was going to sing "O Holy Night"? I am a singer, but I just couldn't do it. My great niece Savannah volunteered and we joined in as the words rang through the night. We have met every year since then except for 2020 when COVID prevented us from gathering. Christmas 2025 was tough because of Gwen's recent passing.

But, for the first time in all of the years these "feral cats" had come together, every family member brought food and drink and their own special memories and we celebrated Gwen's legacy and my mother and father's legacy. One of Gwen's grandsons stopped me as we were leaving and told me how much it meant to meet and keep Gwen's memory alive.

We will do it again. And again. Until I can't sing "O Holy Night" and someone will have to take over!

ABOUT THE AUTHOR

Bruce Hennigan grew up in Northwest Louisiana and became a physician practicing in the field of radiology. He was a church drama director for 15 years and wrote over 150 plays. He is a certified apologist, or one who defends the truthfulness of the Christian faith with Reasons to Believe and with the North American Mission Board in the role of a Certified Apologetic Instructor. He speaks on this topic on a regular basis. Bruce is also the author of nine books in the supernatural thriller series, "The Chronicles of Jonathan Steel" as well as "Death by Darwin", "The Homecoming Tree", "Our Darkness, His Light", and, with Mark Sutton, "Hope Again: A Lifetime Plan for Conquering Depression" and "Shadow Merchant: A Jack Merchant Medical Mystery" as well as "Merchant of Justice, Book 2."

Bruce is married to the most incredible woman in the world, Sherry. They have two adult children and they live in Shreveport, Louisiana. Bruce and Sherry along with their daughter, Casey, are strong advocates of support for epilepsy patients and their caregivers.

For more information on books: hopeagainbooks.com

BOOKS BY BRUCE HENNIGAN

Hope Again: A Lifetime Plan for Conquering Depression (with Mark Sutton)
The Homecoming Tree
Our Darkness, His Light
Shadow Merchant (Book 1 of Jack Merchant Medical Mysteries)
Merchant of Justice (Book 2)
Just a Bite of Something Sweet: At Christmas
The Chronicles of Jonathan Steel:
Death by Darwin (Jonathan Steel Prequel)
Book 1 - Demon 13: Dark Covenant
Book 2 - Demon 12: Wolf Dragon
Book 3 - Demon 11: Ark of the Chimera
Volume 1: The Chronicles of Jonathan Steel (ebook with books 1 - 3)
Book 4 - The 10th Demon: Children of the Bloodstone
Book 5 - The 9th Demon: Time of the Cross
Book 6 - The 8th Demon: A Wicked Numinosity
Volume 2: The Chronicles of Jonathan Steel (ebook with books 4 - 6)

BOOKS BY BRUCE HENNIGAN

Books 7 & 8 - The Pandora Stone: Demons 7, 6 & 5
Book 9 - The 4th Demon: Trial of the 3rd Demon
Book 10 - The 2nd Demon: Tales of the Grimvox
Volume 3: The Chronicles of Jonathan Steel (ebook with books 7 - 10)

www.ingramcontent.com/pod-product-compliance
Lightning Source LLC
Chambersburg PA
CBHW030255100526
44590CB00012B/405